FREEDOM AND ORDER IN THE UNIVERSITY

Freedom and Order in the University

EDITED WITH AN INTRODUCTION BY
SAMUEL GOROVITZ

ESSAYS BY PAUL GOODMAN

WALTER P. METZGER

JOHN R. SEARLE

SANFORD H. KADISH

MORTIMER R. KADISH

The Press of Western Reserve University
1967

69- 04429

To my parents, for giving freedom its due; to Ellen and Peter Sterling and Arthur Waldstein, for knowing a great deal about freedom and order; and, most of all, to daisies—that need air and water and sun and space in order to grow and thrive—for making the world more beautiful.

The significance of freedom lies in the use that is made of it.
                                                    —*Louie Arnaud Reid*

Preface

The material that constitutes the major content of this book was originally delivered in November, 1965, in a symposium on Freedom and Order in the University, sponsored by the WRU–Case Program of Philosophical Studies. The program is a joint undertaking of Western Reserve University and Case Institute of Technology. With the support of the Carnegie Corporation, it conducts, in addition to its graduate study and research activities, various symposia and seminars that focus on issues of interdisciplinary concern; for example, recent seminars have treated moral problems in psychotherapy, philosophy in literature, and the logic of decision in the social sciences. With the symposium on Freedom and Order, the program sponsored for the first time a discussion of genuine relevance to the full spectrum of interests within the university community. Out of the enthusiastic response to the symposium arose the decision to make available a revised and expanded version of the content of the discussions.

Each of the distinguished panelists in this symposium presented a statement of position with regard to the issues in question; each such statement was answered by another of the panel members. The statements and replies were recorded and transcribed, and prior to publication underwent minor revision and polishing. The authors have tried to do maximum justice to their positions, even if at some cost to correspondence with the original remarks, and it is our hope that a better book has resulted. Selected portions of the informal discussions are included where those exchanges are of self-contained interest or of direct relevance to points raised in the initial statements or replies. The final essay was written some months after the symposium; it presents a retrospective view of the positions taken and a reflective discussion of the topic. The editor's introduction, also, has two aspects. The first part contains a discussion of the issues and of the symposium essays that is with some justice called introductory. The second part presents a portion of the editor's own views about the issues in question, and makes some concrete suggestions about the implementation of freedom in universities.

Many people in addition to the contributors have helped in the making of this book, and I wish to acknowledge their aid explicitly. Professors Isaac Levi and David Cohen, and Dean Lester Crocker contributed substantially to the success of the original symposium as commentators from the host institutions. Dean Crocker was also instrumental in encouraging publication of the proceedings, and in arranging for the provision of support from the Western Reserve University Fund for Grants in Aid of Research. A special note of appreciation goes to Ernest Trova, whose gracious contribution of the cover design is a mark of his concern with issues of freedom and constraint in contemporary society. Thanks are due Mr. Bruce Miller for his careful preparation of the annotated bibliography. Finally, I want to thank the American Association of University Professors and the American Civil Liberties Union for permission to reprint their statements as appendices.

S.G.

Cleveland, Ohio
October 1966

Contents

VI

FREEDOM AND ORDER IN THE UNIVERSITY

Introduction

1. Talk of freedom surrounds us. In discussions of political issues we hear that freedom is an overriding political value. When we talk about morality and responsibility, we commonly invoke some concept of personal freedom, holding that a man is responsible for his actions only insofar as he is free to act otherwise. This concern with personal freedom manifests itself in many ways; Dostoevski's man from underground is so obsessed with personal freedom that he willfully acts in flagrant violation of his own interests so as to gain the "most advantageous advantage" of feeling free to act in accordance with whim independently of considerations of prudence. But when we reflect on the meaning of the talk about freedom that we hear in so many different contexts, it becomes plain that the notion of freedom is commonly confused and unclear. In what sense of "freedom" could it be true that *l'homme est né libre?* Free to do what, free in what way?

Man is born helpless; as he grows, gradually, with the aid of others, and to a greater or lesser degree, he gains freedom from some of the constraints and dependences that constitute his initial helplessness. If we wish to make clear sense of talk about freedom, we must note that the concept of freedom is logically relational. Just as it makes no sense to speak of a man as "taller than," without specifying *what* he is "taller than," so too it makes no sense to speak of a man as free or as having freedom without specifying the nature of the constraint with respect to which he is said to be free. Sometimes the context makes the meaning perfectly clear; too often nothing makes the meaning clear at all. Thus, every man is free in some ways, and no man is free in all

1

ways. Every man, Epictetus suggests, is free to approve or disapprove of his lot. And the laws of physics constrain us all.

If we are concerned with freedom in the university, we must reflect on the nature and effect of the various constraints that can inhibit action in a university setting. We must ask what kinds of constraint the university ought to seek to eliminate from its students and faculty in order to make most likely the accomplishment of its objectives and the fulfillment of its obligations. Hence, no discussion of freedom in the university can ignore the need to examine questions about the aims and responsibilities of the institution. Such a discussion should help make clear what kinds of constraint on behavior are relevant to the university's purposes, and in what ways. Constraint on speech, plainly, is just one among many species of constraint that loom large in considerations of university policy. And we cannot ignore the distinction between constraints imposed by the university on its citizens and constraints imposed on the university as an institution by the larger social, political, and economic community of which it is a part. The two issues are of course related in obvious ways. Sometimes a university is not free itself to grant to its citizens certain freedoms that would in fact be conducive to its objectives. But only by recognizing as distinct the question of constraints to which the institution is subject can we properly see the connections between constraints placed on the institution and those placed by it.

The provision of freedom may be construed as taking place primarily in two ways. The university can refrain from imposing constraints on behavior of some specific kind. For example, the policy may be adopted that student groups may invite and hear any speaker whatsoever at the university. This sort of freedom is the result of the institution deciding against, or simply failing to impose, rules, sanctions, and penalties that it might have otherwise imposed or sought to impose. Call this a negative conception of freedom; it parallels the nature of the concept of political freedom in thirteenth-century England. Political freedom then was considered to be enjoyed when the state did not tell the citizens not to do what they might otherwise do. But there is a second, positive way in which freedom may be provided by an institution, and that is through the effort to remove constraints that would otherwise be present. This more active conception of providing freedom is reflected in the principles of the "Great Society." The government undertakes as within its right and responsibility the elimination of constraints imposed upon citizens by non-governmental influences. A simple illustration is federal aid to depressed areas; such aid aims to increase the capacity of its recipients to live in keeping with broadly accepted values by lifting from their shoulders the constraints of poverty and lack of economic and educational opportunity. The university, too, can provide freedom in this more active way, by opposing constraints on the behavior of its citizens that are not of its own imposition.

I suggest, then, that it may be of use to view the entire discussion of freedom and order in the university with the following questions in mind. What sorts of constraints ought the university impose and for what reasons? What sorts ought to be tolerated? What kinds of constraints should the university oppose by refraining from imposing them even under internal or external pressure to do so? What kinds should the university oppose by engaging in active attempts to remove them where they exist? And the answers, I suggest, depend upon what the objectives and obligations of the university are taken to be. Indeed, only with respect to a position about the objectives and obligations of the institution can answers to such questions be justified at all.

If we hold that the aim of the university is to educate people, with a primary view toward their own development and self-fulfillment, we find the student freedoms conducive to that end differ somewhat from those most conducive to the kind of training which places primary emphasis on the graduate's suitability to play well-defined roles in a well-established industrial society. If we view the university as under an obligation to support the values and satisfy the occupational needs of the society that surrounds it, we discover that a different conception of academic freedom is appropriate from that which suits a university that sees as an essential feature of its obligations the support and fostering of incisive social criticism.

2. On October 2, 1964, Mario Savio stood atop a police car on the Berkeley campus of the University of California, surrounded by thousands of students, and publicly served notice that the

Berkeley Free Speech Movement would continue direct action until the university administration yielded to its demands. Student demonstration, by that time, was nothing new. The civil rights movement had already made major demonstrations a frequent characteristic of the national scene, and, all along, students had played a key role in that movement. But the demonstration at Berkeley was, all the same, something new. It lasted thirty-two hours, and virtually brought to a halt the workings of one of the country's most prestigious academic institutions. And in the end, the university made major concessions in the direction of removing constraints previously placed on the dissemination of ideas on the Berkeley campus. The student demonstrators, supported by a significant percentage of the rest of the student community, had achieved their objectives.

Since that October, the events at Berkeley have stimulated numerous discussions and a flood of published comment. Degrees of blame have been assigned to all sides of the conflict. In the public view, however, the student demonstrators are to a large degree the primary villains. And the revolution at Berkeley has had consequences all over the country. For the first time in the recent history of American higher education, significant numbers of students believe that they are in a position to translate their discontents into demands and to back up their demands with a show of power that, even in the absence of relevant authority, must be heeded. But, we are constantly reminded, order must be preserved. When students demonstrate for greater freedom of one sort or another, they must do so in orderly fashion. And the response to their demands must leave the university still in a position to maintain order. Thus there seems to be in fact a natural tension between the demands of the freedom-seeking students and the commitment to order of the administrators, trustees, alumni, and neighbors of universities, and of those who are responsible for public educational systems. Out of this tension arose the conflict at Berkeley; and out of this tension arises the need for a discussion of freedom and order that goes beyond the particulars of the Berkeley Revolution.

All four of the major contributors to this discussion had first-hand experience with the crisis at Berkeley. Sanford Kadish and

John Searle were deeply involved throughout, and Paul Goodman and Walter Metzger both made visits to the campus. In addition, Paul Goodman was considered the ideological patron saint of the Free Speech Movement. Nonetheless, with the exception of John Searle, the contributors do not discuss the Berkeley situation with any special emphasis; rather, they draw on their experience and understanding of what happened to go beyond that situation to broader concerns. And, although John Searle does discuss in detail certain features of the crisis, he explicitly does so in the context of seeking broadly applicable guidelines for dealing with problems of freedom and order.

All of the issues mentioned above arise in the ensuing discussions, although for the most part they are not so much treated explicitly as they are woven into the fabric of the dialogue. The positions developed share broad agreement about the objectives and obligations of the university, and all the contributors value the aim of providing students and faculty with the maximum amount of freedom to grow and develop that is compatible with the constraints imposed by the need for order. Yet in no sense do they speak with a single voice. On the contrary, their positions range over a broad spectrum, from the admittedly anarchistic stance assumed by Paul Goodman, who argues that the only defensible order is that which arises naturally out of total freedom, to the legalistic defense of behavior-governing rules offered by Sanford Kadish. As a result, sharp disagreements emerge.

3. Goodman begins the discussion by arguing that maximum freedom is not only conducive to, but essential for, genuine education; that the order imposed by present administrators, indeed by the very educational systems they administer, is a deterrent to such freedom and hence to education; and that the structure of present educational institutions should therefore be dissolved, making possible a regrouping of interests along natural and self-motivated lines. Only then will what goes on in universities be relevant to the human development of their students as people and citizens. Goodman's position is, by his own admission, extreme, and it provokes in many quarters the kind of astonished disdain that commonly greets extreme views. To be sure, Goodman's lack of respect for the role of administrators is so unquali-

fied as to give pause even to the most harassed victims of the sometimes mysterious ways of presidents, provosts, chancellors, and deans, and the regulation-bound clerks and functionaries that surround them. For it seems plain all the same that some of what administrators do must be done and that if such tasks were left to faculty members, the necessity of performing them would be viewed as an infringement on the scholar's freedom to pursue his own interests. But it is too easy simply to dismiss Goodman's views as the dreams of a naive visionary. He is one of those rare individuals who combine a keen sensitivity to the influence on human beings of what he sees going on around him with an unqualified willingness to shout "Naked!" when he sees an emperor with no clothes. And time and time again, when we take a second look after hearing his shout, we also notice that something is indeed very wrong.

Weaknesses in some of Goodman's arguments will be apparent, and practical objections to his suggestions will be legion. A number are well raised by Sanford Kadish in his reply. We need not dwell on them. It is not that we should be unaware of weaknesses in Goodman's remarks; rather we should be aware that we do this eleutheromaniac evangelist an injustice—and possibly ourselves more so—if we view him and evaluate him as a practical educator. His proposals are untempered by the harsh realities of practical considerations because he *refuses* to worry about practical considerations. Such refusal, moreover, makes perfectly good sense; there is no risk at all that insufficient attention will be paid to the demands of practicality. Far from being the result of a genuine naiveté, Goodman's refusal to face the problems of practicality is a consistent reflection of his view that many people are concerned with too little else. To see that this is so, one need only observe the architectural atrocities that often result from the fact that the decisions about university building are so substantially influenced by very practical people, who often fail to realize that environmental beauty makes a difference to education. One can well imagine the benefit of giving a voice in such planning to a man whose *single-minded* concern is with aesthetic values. Similarly, even those who recoil at the thought of giving Goodman his way should be able to recognize the value of giving such a spokesman a fair hearing.

Admittedly, it is unthinkable that we take the university and "just let it fall apart" as Goodman suggests. But universities do suffer, sometimes to a startling degree, from inflexibilities that arise out of the inevitable bureaucracy that exists to support, but takes on a life of its own within, any large and complex institution. Of course we cannot eliminate the structure within the university. But we can keep in mind, more than we do, the obvious and oft-neglected truth that learners and teachers are what universities are for; and it sometimes takes the striking claims of Paul Goodman to emphasize the extent to which such simple truths become submerged and forgotten as the functioning of a university becomes more and more dictated by the structure entrenched within it. Norbert Wiener was fond of citing the example of a business-man whose activities were constrained by the limitations of the bookkeeping system he adopted to keep a record of his activities. The same phenomenon occurs in universities, and it is in order to eliminate such constraints on action that Goodman argues for elimination of the structure that can constrain. His discussion of the efficacy of, and interrelationships among, the various levels of our present educational establishment argues well that in many ways the accepted patterns of education can fruitfully be challenged and reappraised at more fundamental levels than is common even among most of the more active contemporary educational reformers.

Walter Metzger provides in his initial remarks an eloquent historical account of the development of the traditional American conception of academic freedom, and he argues that American universities, unlike the German universities by which they were largely influenced, restricted the application of academic freedom exclusively to faculty members. After discussing the factors that account for this restriction, Metzger goes on to characterize academic freedom as having five basic components: classroom autonomy for the teacher, tenure protection for the qualified, freedom of inquiry for the scholar, extramural freedom for the staff member, and due process for the accused. The first two components are plainly not relevant to students, but the next three, Metzger argues, can and should be extended to include students. As indicative of the traditional restriction of the concept of academic freedom to faculty members, he cites the total absence of any mention of student rights in the American Association of University Professors statement on academic freedom. But the A.A.U.P. has now published its position on the academic freedom of students.[1] In that statement freedom of thought, discussion, and inquiry, freedom from university interference in restriction of extramural activity, and due process in disciplinary proceedings are emphasized. Thus, the mending of the rift for which Metzger hopes is underway, and although the gap is undeniable between an A.A.U.P. statement of policy on the one hand and the widespread adoption of such policy on the other, still the direction of change is clear and the extension of academic freedom to students is more and more universally becoming a reality.

John Searle, in his reply to Metzger, agrees entirely with Metzger's plea for extension; he suggests that the ideological battle, at least at Berkeley, is won; and he expresses a desire to turn to problems of interpretation and implementation of that victory. He goes on to argue that the fight at Berkeley was about more than what Metzger seems to suggest is called for,[2] and begins to espouse the positive or "maximalist" conception of freedom that he discusses further in his own paper.

It would, of course, be unwarranted to infer from the changes which have occurred at the University of California that greatly expanded freedom of action now generally comes with every student identification card at every school. Rather, places like Berkeley serve to set the pace and direction, with changes at other and particularly smaller schools coming piecemeal and sporadically as the trend to liberalization of student-governing rules spreads. The newspapers seem often to give the impression that it is merely a question of time, and very little at that, before standards of student freedom across the country satisfy the demands of the FSM. We read that at San Francisco State the students now control a faculty appointment, at Stanford undergraduates over

[1] See Appendix I, where the A.A.U.P. statement is reprinted.
[2] For an excellent discussion of what the FSM revolution was about, see: Seymour M. Lipset and Sheldon S. Wolin, *The Berkeley Student Revolt*, Garden City: Doubleday Anchor, 1965.

twenty-one are subject to no university restrictions on their posses-
sion and use of alcohol, at Yale student protests have prompted
reconsideration of a tenure decision, and at Wayne State the
president has defied the state legislature's prohibition of Communist speakers on campus. But at hundreds of junior colleges and
colleges, and at many universities, life goes on as ever. Students,
faculty, and administrators perhaps read with interest of events
and conditions at other schools, but substantial change is seldom
achieved and often not even seriously sought. There is a new wave
of student freedom, but it will sweep back and forth across the
nation many times before the student populace in general becomes
immersed. We can therefore look to Berkeley as a precursor of
things to come. The demands made by students at Berkeley have
been echoed elsewhere, and some of the changes made at Berkeley
are being made elsewhere. Similarly, the problems that arise at
Berkeley foreshadow problems that others will face with extra-
university influences such as the police, the politicians, and the
public, and with the internal workings of new ways of adjudicating
the conflicting student, faculty, and administration interests. In a
sense, then, the Berkeley campus has done much more than force
into prominence a host of questions about freedom and order in
the university. It has become in fact a massive laboratory for the
testing of answers to such questions.

There have been battles about student freedom before and
elsewhere, and there have been campuses, such as Antioch and
Bennington, long renowned for the high degree of student freedom they provide. The real impact of the changes at Berkeley
stems from its status as a massive, state-supported school whose
quality by many commonly respected criteria is extremely high.
Recently rated as having the finest graduate school in the country,[3] Berkeley is widely viewed as a paradigm of what the ever
growing state-supported school should be, and its academic excellence is respected universally by the best of the private universities
as well. When many students in such a school rise up in revolt, it
is no wonder that the countless admirers of that place are given
pause.

[3] Allan M. Carter, *An Assessment of Quality in Graduate Education*, Washington: American Council on Education, 1966.

John Searle was an ardent supporter of the FSM, and he knows what happened at Berkeley not just from being there but from being in the midst of those happenings. He is now Special Assistant to the Chancellor for Student Organization and is largely responsible for the implementation of the policies he supported during the revolution. Thus he can no longer afford to indulge in the purity of Goodmanian vision. Such vision perhaps sets the direction; Searle must now hack out a path through the jungle of practical complications within an existing structure. Some of the Berkeleyites thus view him as a defector to the administration, while other, more temperate observers view his presence in the administration as a major victory for the cause of student freedom.[4]

Searle begins his discussion by accepting teaching and research as the objectives of the university. But he rejects what he calls the "minimalist" view of academic freedom—the view that the justification of academic freedom is its importance for the attainment of those objectives. Rather, Searle defends the "maximalist" theory of freedom, which takes freedom for granted and holds that any restrictions on freedom are what must be justified in terms of the objectives of the university. He then goes on to discuss the emergence at Berkeley of a change in policy in the direction of the maximalist theory of freedom. But such a theory leaves the university open to difficulties of many sorts—there are constant challenges to any constraints the administration seeks to justify and impose; the amount of activity engendered by the high degree of freedom at times seems to threaten the tranquillity demanded by scholarship; the influence of non-students on campus activities is hard to evaluate or control; and the public responds antagonistically to many manifestations of the new freedom. But, Searle says, the defenders of the maximalist theory mean business—in full awareness of the problems they face, they mean to live by two ideals: that the university does not in any way restrict the content of speech, and that the only acceptable constraints on freedom are those that are necessary for the protection of the normal function's of the university. One way to defend these ideals in spite of the problems that arise may be to provide for the assimilation of student activism into the university curriculum, but such a pro-

[4] Cf. Herbert Gold, "I am a U.C. student—do not fold, bend or mutilate," *The Saturday Evening Post*, June 18, 1966.

gram has its own limitations and pitfalls. In the end, no simple formulas will suffice for the implementation of an orderly freedom. Rather, each situation will have to be judged on its merits, and the battle against betrayal of the ideal by the adoption of expedient but avoidable regulations must be fought untiringly.

Walter Metzger, in reply, expresses substantial basic agreement, but disputes a number of subsidiary points. He defends the FSM as an intellectual movement, contrary to Searle's suggestion, and he rejects Searle's construal of the A.A.U.P. notion of academic freedom as being deficient in breadth of conception. He then concludes with some observations about the significance of the fact that the student revolution took place at Berkeley.

Of course Searle has not adopted the extreme position, defended by Goodman, that all or very nearly all rules are avoidable and that a community of free spirits left to its own devices will work out patterns of behavior that will enhance the value of the lives in the community. Rather, he seeks to minimize rules in recognition that some must be retained for the protection of the university as a viable institution. Goodman might well be happy to agree, arguing that the necessity of rules to protect the functioning of the institution merely supports his contention that the functioning of that institution is illegitimate. But if we are concerned with freedom and order within the university, then presumably we will share Searle's commitment to the university as a valuable institution. We can agree that our universities play an exaggerated or partially misdirected role in the education of our youth. And we can decry their many flaws. Still, we will not fail to recognize the need for some means of ensuring enough order in the university to permit both normal functioning and improvement.

Sanford Kadish addresses his remarks to questions concerning the form and function that the unavoidable regulations may take. He begins by pointing out that rules have, in addition to their "tough" side that preserves order, a "benign" side that serves the interests of freedom. When we wish to give the benign side its due in establishing a set of rules, five areas of questions arise. We must first ask what sorts of behavior may appropriately be constrained. Second, we must decide what sorts of regulations, formulated with what degree of precision, are suitable to the context. Even with these issues settled, we still need to establish enforcement procedures, and our concern with due process will be reflected in the enforcement procedures we adopt. Fourth, we must determine a range of sanctions, for in the absence of sanctions rules become merely optional guidelines. The range of sanctions within the university is characteristically sharply limited, and the system of rules thus lacks the essential flexibility of rules backed by, say, a sliding scale of fines. Fifth, the question that underlies all of these issues must be faced, and its consideration is in a sense propaedeutic to consideration of the other four. Some decisions must be made about how questions in the four above-mentioned areas are to be answered. Kadish declines to answer these questions, suggesting that the answers will emerge gradually as a result of the sort of experimentation that is typified by John Searle's administrative activities. He then turns his attention specifically to questions of the first sort, concerning what kinds of behavior it is appropriate for the university to constrain. Such constraint, he holds, is justified only when the university has a "legitimate regulatory concern" with behavior of the kind in question. And what one accepts as a legitimate regulatory concern will depend on what one takes to be the proper functions and purposes of the university.

Goodman, in response, allows that rules, ideally of a "common law" sort, have a legitimate place in society, but holds that there is a distinction between enforcement and sanction and argues that rules should be enforced without sanction. He then argues against Kadish's claim that some kinds of situations call for restriction on the content of speech, denying that even cheating on examinations falls within the university's proper regulative domain. He concludes that, in addition to permitting on-campus advocacy of illegal off-campus activity, the university should intercede in behalf of its own citizens who run afoul of the law off campus.

Following each essay and reply is a selection of the remarks made in discussion at the symposium. These remarks have been heavily edited, and rearranged. Although for purposes of publication they seem to cluster most naturally around Essays I and II, this does not accurately reflect the temporal sequence of the actual discussions.

In the final essay, Mortimer R. Kadish rounds out the discussion with "Reflections on the Nature of the Problem." He begins by arguing that some of the symposiasts formulate the problem of

providing order in the university in terms that misleadingly prejudice the issues in advance. He examines the approach of each of
the four essayists in turn, and concludes that key issues concerning
the logic of the problem are not adequately clarified in the preceding discussions. Kadish then offers an analysis of the problem
of maintaining order, arguing that the problem has political and
"cognitive" aspects, and that these aspects can most fruitfully be
viewed from a decision-theoretic approach, in terms of possible
alternative courses of action and an assessment of the goals,
probabilities of success, and costs of each alternative. He concludes
with a section on the limits that any solution to such a complex
problem must face, such limits insuring that the problem will
constitute an ever present challenge to our universities.

II. THE LIBERATING UNIVERSITY

1. Universities today do many things; they train, educate, facilitate
the conduct of research, provide a forum for the exchange of ideas
and hence for the development of social criticism, and provide a
haven and a livelihood for valuable people who in other circumstances might be forced to sacrifice a portion, perhaps a large
portion, of their value—poets, artists, philosophers, social critics,
etc. These are all legitimate and important functions, some of
which more specifically call for a university setting than others.
The two that are central, however, are training and education, and
the distinction between them can hardly be emphasized enough.

It is demonstrably possible for a person to go through virtually
any college in the country and emerge, degree in hand, essentially
untouched by education—and possibly quite well trained. Education involves a great deal more than training—that is, than skill—
be it the ability to design a product, write a brief, or remove an
appendix.[5] As people become better educated, they become in-

[5] Walter Lippmann recently made the point this way: "There is more to
the task of learning than to discover more and more truths than have ever been
known before. That something more, which may mark the difference between
mediocrity and excellence, is the practice of a kind of alchemy, the creative
function of transmuting knowledge into wisdom. . . . The capacity to judge
rightly in a choice of both means and ends cuts across the specialties and the
technologies, and it is, I dare to say, the hallmark of a liberal, as distinguished
from a utilitarian or vocational, education" ("The University," *The New
Republic*, May 28, 1966).

creasingly concerned with issues that bear no immediate practical impact on their lives. Just as an appreciation of Wordsworth is a product of education, so too is an appreciation of the plight of others and an eagerness to partake open-mindedly in the exchange of ideas. Such appreciation and eagerness lead naturally to concern with the deficiencies of the environment we inhabit; the educated man will see the failings as well as the virtues in his society and, even if not active in its initiation, will be responsive to informed and responsible social criticism. Moreover, the facts of contemporary life, especially of contemporary urban American life, make social criticism unavoidable among the intelligent—and the university is one of the leading gathering places of the intelligent. Social criticism, then, arises predictably in our universities, and its vigor may be viewed as one mark of the quality of education and the vitality of the exchange of ideas at a university. In addition, incisive social criticism and the sort of intellectual awareness and openness out of which it arises are primary and possibly essential means to education.

No one questions the importance of the university as an institution of training. But as Paul Goodman and others point out, it is unnecessary, even undesirable, for the university to be the exclusive or paradigmatic locus even of sophisticated training. Education, too, is possible outside the university—indeed, the university can at most be a spur to the process. The ideally educated man is a man who always and everywhere is—who perhaps cannot help but be—continuing to grow and learn from all that surrounds him. Social criticism and the open exchange of ideas, also, can and do take place outside the university. But there are special reasons why the university is particularly well suited to the fostering of social criticism, and why it should be inherently an unconstrained and unconstraining institution. Education, as opposed to mere training, is a process that heightens awareness, encourages openness, and promotes the development of durable intellectual concerns. It can take place only in an open environment among educated people. In keeping with its objective of providing education, the university must maintain the sort of atmosphere that encourages heightened sensitivity to the environment and critical consideration of what men do in and to it.

In addition to being of pedagogical value, social criticism is of enormous value to the society against which it is directed. As John Fischer wrote recently:

> What this country needs is radicals who will stay that way—regardless of the creeping years, the inevitable blunders, defeats, and combat fatigue. For the rate of change in the world today is unimaginably faster than ever before, and we can hope to survive in reasonably good shape only if we change our human institutions fast enough to keep up. This means constant radical reexamination of everything in sight, from political systems to sex habits—radical in the old sense of going to the roots. How long can anybody hope for a decent life, for example, if we keep doubling the earth's population every forty years? Do our old political boundaries make any sense when a single city sprawls across three states? The list of such questions is endless—and you can be sure that the conservatives won't even ask them, much less find the answers.[6]

Such individuals are indeed needed, and the university—because, at least in principle, it can be fairly well isolated from external pressures and influences—logically is the institution to nurture them and their ideas. Conformity is both a danger of democracy and a danger to democracy; non-conformity of the desirable and essential kinds, like that of the innocuous or harmful kinds, thrives only in a tolerant, flexible environment—the sort the university, functioning as it should with a minimum of constraint, almost alone can provide. As Lawrence Cremin writes:

> I should like to reiterate Beard's dictum that a democratic society should support schools which must then be left free to criticize the society that supports them. There is an ever present danger in the popular control of popular education, which Tocqueville called "the tyranny of the majority"—the insistence upon uniformity and acceptability of ideas and the insistence upon service to society in its narrowest, most utilitarian sense. To the extent that such tyranny prevails, popular education ceases to be education and becomes indoctrination in the commonest popular prejudices. Academic freedom is the public protection against such cheapening; and it must be

[6] John Fischer, "Letter to a New Leftist, From a Tired Liberal," *Harper's Magazine*, March 1966, p. 16.

encouraged not merely because it befits scholars but because it benefits the society that sustains it. This, of course, means tension, for given academic freedom no public relations effort on the part of educational administrators can obscure the conflict of ideas and ideals that will result. In the end, the democrat is sustained by the faith that such conflict is generally incident to the search for truth, beauty, and goodness. His opponents, who value order and uniformity above all things, will doubtless get more tranquil but less educative schools.[7]

The double value of social criticism, as educative and as socially therapeutic, calls for an enlightened and active implementation within the university of a commitment to freedom. If the university is to provide an environment in which social criticism can thrive, it must be dedicated to freedom—for itself as an institution and for its citizens—from the constraints of traditional values and social pressures, as well as from economic interests. It must provide its students with freedom to grow and learn not just about a professional or academic discipline, but about themselves and their world. This is possible only when there is a serious emphasis on education, independent of training. In this era when we know so impressively well how to do things, and handle so appallingly badly the questions of whether and what to do, when our skill has left wisdom so far behind as to be almost out of view, we need more flexible, inventive, active, and open-minded individuals. Yet the current emphasis on schooling, and, for the most part, the practical consequences of that emphasis, serve to increase the pressure on teachers to train, and on students to be trained for, what is ostensibly utility in the practical affairs of society. The purported emphasis on education has in fact been in the main an emphasis on training, and that emphasis is reflected in myriad ways on campuses across the nation.

One might expect that as a result of such emphasis the student populace would exhibit a decrease in social consciousness and activism. But the opposite has been the case. As the pressure to train for utility increases, so, fortunately, do the ranks of students who will not submit to such pressure. It is true that the student

[7] Lawrence S. Cremin, *The Genius of American Education*, Pittsburgh: University of Pittsburgh Press, 1965, pp. 107–8.

who, training to become a doctor or engineer or lawyer, is too busy and single minded to reflect on the problems that face his fellow man and ultimately himself, is also a student who is not likely to be moved to action in the name of social progress or educational reform. The student who is discontent, uncertain about his future, or alienated from the direction in which he sees civilization developing is a student who is much more likely to take action. Thus it should come as no surprise that student activists come more from the liberal arts than from the sciences and preprofessional programs, are more likely to be malcontents than those who envision for themselves a particular niche in society, are more often the educated than the merely trained. But it would be a mistake to measure the appropriateness of protest by evaluating the coherence, organization, or appearance of the protesters. Granted that student activism most noticeably takes the form of protest, and all too often of indiscriminate, uninformed, and nonconstructive protest. Still, the point is not that the need to protest is illusory because the protesters seem a strange bunch. On the contrary, although to a large extent the protesters are a strange bunch—strange at least in their active opposition to the targets of their protest—their activities would not seem so strange if more people recognized the awesome need for informed social criticism translated into considered action.

The revolution at Berkeley was not just about freedom of speech or political action. As much as anything, it was about the emphasis on training. The Berkeley students are young, energetic, bright, individualistic, and sensitive; they were aware that the constraints placed on freedom of expression by regulations limiting the use of Bancroft Strip had a significance that went beyond the question of free speech to the broader question of the kind of environment that is required by commitment to education. They felt, in large numbers, as if they were being processed by a massive mechanism for training, while a pretense of liberal education was maintained by an elusive academic power structure to which they seemingly had no access. The FSM revolt could not have been carried to success by the FSM members alone. It was a success because students by the thousand saw and seized an opportunity to ventilate their alienation from the university and the social, economic, and political establishments it seemed to represent.[8] They wanted an education, and, though they perhaps did not know explicitly what was lacking, they knew that an education called for something more than what the university seemed to be providing. A part of that something more is what John Searle speaks about in his espousal of a maximalist theory of freedom on the campus. And insight into that something more is shown by Joseph Katz and Nevitt Sanford, who write:

> It is our view, one that is well-supported in psychological theory, that the person is all of a piece, that intellectual, emotional, and characterological processes develop in interaction one with another.
>
> It follows from this that where our aim is to produce scholars our major effort should be to create a community of scholars, offer the student clear and attractive models of scholarship, deliberately build his confidence in his ability to become a scholar, and give him freedom to be guided in his intellectual work by his curiosity.
>
> Where our aim, in addition to producing scholars, is to produce educated men and women, possessed of such qualities as independence of thinking, the ability to make wise choices, social responsibility, taste and sensibility, and sensitivity to the feelings of others, we must learn to use the intellectual offerings of the college in new ways. We must know what students are like and relate what goes on in the classroom to their needs and

[8] One student's sense of alienation is well captured by Robert Coles's report of the student's remarks: "I don't know whether I'm ready to face that business, again: the pompous self-righteous officials, noisy with worry about orgasms in young people, but discreetly silent when we are sent off to war to kill or be killed; full of reminders about how moral we must be, and responsible to others, not just ourselves, but without a word of concern about the immorality of the slums next door, or the dishonest intrigue we've practiced in the Caribbean or elsewhere. They go so very easily from our sexual habits to the broadest conclusions about our honor and our generation's character, but they don't welcome a look at their honor. A person's political views are private, they tell you; but our views on sex not only aren't private but are fair game for anybody's use—to call us every name in the book. If I wear a beard and a girl I love stays in my room all night and I sleep ⸱ith her, I'm a beatnik and in a state of moral decline. If I shave and go to a whore house, buy stocks on the South African exchange that net me a large profit, and sign up for the CIA when I graduate from college, my behavior is unquestioned and my integrity assumed" (*The New Republic*, May 28, 1966, p. 21).

concerns. We must challenge what they believe most firmly, discuss what they are most passionate about, give them the means for analyzing their nonrational behavior, show them how they can do well what they most want to do.[9]

If we are to meet the challenge and provide an environment for education in our universities, and if we accept the view that the university as an institution has a serious obligation to a disinterested search for truth, including truth about the deficiencies of the society that supports the institution, then we must ask what kinds of constraint on behavior interfere with the pursuit of these goals, and we must work to eliminate those constraints regardless of their origin. Independently of its prima-facie value, freedom in the university is a necessary condition for the proper business of the university.

2. Constraints on behavior can arise from any aspect of life, and an exhaustive examination of their operation in a university setting would require a major work. Students and faculty can obviously be bound by economic, social, and political constraints. In addition, their freedom of action can be limited by physical, temporal, moral, legal, psychological, and academic constraints. A particularly common and inadequately recognized source of constraint, finally, arises from various sorts of lack of opportunity and exposure. Here we can but briefly make some illustrative observations about some of these constraints, and can offer a few suggestions for their reduction.

(a) A common sort of complaint at Berkeley and other large universities concerns a cluster of issues often referred to as lack of access to the administration. The student who has a complaint or a suggestion for change, or who is charged with some offense, is at a loss to pursue his cause effectively in the absence of explicit and readily available information about the policies and procedures in force at the university. Thus a frequent student demand is for administration publication of comprehensive and unequivocal regulations. But the administration never complies, and the lack of compliance is easily understood. An administration that publishes rules is bound by those rules. It then loses a flexibility that when

[9] Joseph Katz and Nevitt Sanford, "17 to 22: The Turbulent Years," in *Stanford Today*, January 1966, Publications Service of Stanford University.

present could be used wisely and benevolently. Further, the compilation of exhaustive rules is impossible. The scope and variety of problems that arise within a university cannot be anticipated even by one who would be willing to accept the constraint of exhaustive regulations. Finally, the diffusion of authority within the administration is a standard feature of bureaucratic decision making. When it is hard to pinpoint the origin of a decision it is hard to contest that decision effectively or to lay blame at an appropriate door. There is thus some convenience and some safety in the elusiveness of university administrative decisions. The student with a grievance is constrained by ignorance about such procedures and by an inherent elusiveness in the procedures themselves. His plight is often akin to that of the citizen trying to "fight City Hall."

The analogy between the grievance of a student and the grievance of a citizen against his government prompts a suggestion for one way of implementing due process in the university and of giving the student a greater voice in his own affairs. The university could appoint an "ombudsman" charged with the sole responsibility of championing the cause of student complaints and suggestions. He might be hired by a committee of the faculty senate, and should have no superior in the administration, nor any voice in the formation of rules or policies. But he should be thoroughly informed about the university's policies, precedents, vaguenesses, channels of communication, procedures for change, and loci of authority and responsibility—in short, he should know the workings of the university as few others do, and as students almost never can, and he should make available that knowledge for the championing of student interests.

An academic ombudsman could be of great help to students, especially to the student who lacks the confidence and aggressiveness to take up the cudgels on his own. The ombudsman would not be a buffer between student and administration, nor a liaison, but a non-judgmental pilot who would guide each student's efforts through the most effective channels. This system could also be a help to the administration, cutting down on ill-directed assaults not to spare the deans, but to focus complaint and suggestion most appropriately.

(b) Economic constraints on student and faculty freedom are widely recognized. The student who cannot meet the bill cannot gain the education, and the institution of academic financial aid represents effort to reduce economic constraints on the poor but able student. It is also recognized that the faculty member who, for economic reasons, must spend part of his time in non-academic pursuits is that much less free to engage in academic pursuits and is correspondingly less likely to thrive as a teacher, scholar, or artist. But we have not gone far enough. The day does seem to be approaching when no able student will for economic reasons be denied a college education, but even when it comes the scholarship student may remain less likely than other students to benefit from the enrichment of spending his college years in residence. We need more financial aid, and as the cost of education continues to soar we will need increasingly more. In addition, although faculty salaries have increased significantly, economic constraints still inhibit the scholars' work.

Traditionally, it was the business of the university—of the administrators—to raise money and to dispense it judiciously within the university. With the arrival of major foundational sources of support, a large part of the burden of fund raising has shifted to departments and even to individual faculty members. Such a shift, and the greater availability of funds that it accompanies, has many advantages. But it has pitfalls as well. The academic entrepreneur is by now an oft and deservedly satirized character. In some quarters grantsmanship has become an activity practiced and too often respected independently of teaching or research. What is perhaps more serious, the common procedures for the provision of grants are themselves constraining. Scholars and teachers, whatever else they may be, are members of an economic society just like everyone else. The pressure on a faculty member to partake of readily available research funds can not often be resisted. But the funds in general are not awarded on the basis of past performance or future promise independently of a project proposal. The academician is therefore pressured to plan his work in light of the predilections of the coffer guardians. The philosopher whose interests cover problems in the philosophy of science and problems in ethics is pressured to work on the former by the greater availability of funds for such work. The poet or art historian is a second-class citizen in the world of grants, and the academician of any stripe who wants the summer free for reflection, thought about his courses and the direction of his own creative work, and exploration of new directions must all too often subsidize such activity himself, if he can, or forgo it, if he cannot. Yet such a summer may well provide greater benefit to the teacher, his university, and society generally, than a summer spent on a more typical "research project." Here, then, is an illustration of the detrimental influence of one kind of subtle economic constraint. One very sketchy suggestion for its reduction: Make a significantly increased amount of money available for what might best be called "development" grants. Let these grants be financed by new funds or, if necessary, by reallocation of a portion of currently available research funds. Let the grants be awarded, independently of any specific project plans, on the basis of past performance as a scholar, teaching effectiveness, and general contribution to the educational community.

(c) Social and political constraints—often hard to separate—seem to be diminishing in influence at many universities, but such constraints, even where diminished, tend to reappear whenever the opposition to them wanes. At many schools students now enjoy complete freedom to hear speakers of their choice, yet within the last year the Michigan legislature supported a ban on Communist speakers at state-supported campuses, and similar legislation in North Carolina is still in force, even though its effect has been somewhat mitigated by the vesting in the chancellors of the various campuses the authority for decisions about invoking the law. We must not forget, in considering the Berkeley end of the liberality continuum, that there is another end, also, near which thousands of students and faculty members spend their time. The ideological battle may indeed be won, as Searle says, but news of the victory has seemingly not reached Bob Jones University, whose president recently said, "We do not believe it is a just use of the term 'academic freedom' for a man to be able to say, "I'm gonna teach evolution or free love in this school.' Academic freedom here boils down to the ability to say or do anything you want to do—so long as it doesn't offend the Bible."[10]

[10] Quoted by Larry L. King, Harper's Magazine, June 1966.

There is a less obvious and perhaps more pernicious sort of social constraint operant on students that is harder to evaluate and harder to combat prudently. Students enter college in a variety of states: some in the midst of more or less adolescent rebellion, some firmly committed to the values of their background environment, some wholly adrift on a sea of conflicting values. Part of the process of education involves enabling these students to arrive at a value structure that is genuinely their own, and this involves encouraging them, helping them, sometimes forcing them to look at the values they have accepted in the past and those they espouse in the present in a critical and open-minded way. The student must be freed, at least for the purposes of inquiry, from the constraints of the prevailing order of social values. We accomplish this, as Katz and Sanford suggest, by challenging what the student most firmly believes, by "shaking his faith." (And we ought be no gentler with the sophisticated student activist who has himself rejected prevalent social and political values. He, too, can benefit from the need to defend his position.)

How can this sort of education be facilitated? One way, of course, is continuation of the tradition of Socratic dialogue. A new suggestion arises out of the formation of a student protest group at Ohio State University to hunt for something to be against. The protester in search of a cause exhibits a symptomatic discontent; his inarticulate dissatisfactions may ultimately rest on idiosyncratic psychological difficulties, or they may rest on a well-warranted alienation from his surroundings. When someone doesn't "fit in," we must always remember to consider the possibility that there is something wrong with what he is being asked to fit into. But there is another point here. Protest, in addition to being appropriate sometimes, is also sometimes a healthy process as viewed independently of any success being made toward the ostensible goals of the protest. One way to improve a society is to have citizens aware of its flaws as well as its virtues. One way to teach people to see flaws as well as virtues is to involve them in an active way in social criticism. One way to involve a student actively in social criticism, and thus to heighten his social awareness, is to send him off in search of something to protest!

Our college teachers characteristically tend to business in the classroom; if they are concerned about the students' overall development they frequently rely on a vague notion of "the college experience" to provide for such development, and they trust to others—on curriculum committees and lecture-series committees, for example—to handle the particulars. Not so the participants in the teach-in movement; they were explicitly concerned with supplementing the students' classroom fare with a broader educational menu. But the teach-in movement is a partisan movement, which in origin was a specifically directed protest demonstration. What is needed is some non-partisan analogue—an on-going vehicle for high-level criticism that transcends the confines of course, curriculum, and classroom. The suggestion, then, is this: Do not oppose protest and social criticism, but incorporate it— embrace it as a proper and valuable part of an educative environment.

The objection has perhaps already arisen: Protest and criticism once institutionalized cease to be free, unvested, and unconstrained. There is no reason why this need be so, although in a particular case it surely could be so. The incorporation could take many forms. Two crudely sketched possibilities are: first, establishment of a free-wheeling course, required of undergraduates, with no grading, perhaps a sequence of teachers from various departments, and small enough classes to permit sustained active interplay of the sort that would involve each student for a substantial portion of the time; and, second, long-term university support, with no privileges of censorship or review, of a non-partisan counterpart to a teach-in committee—composed of faculty and students, and dedicated to the pursuit of responsible and informed criticism of the university, of the government, of the course of civilization, of whatever there is to examine critically.

Such a move might provide an outlet for the energies of the rebel in search of a cause; in addition it could serve to help with a bigger problem than activism—and that is apathy among the less visible but probably more numerous students who are not tuned in to the greater world around them. As Katz and Sanford write:

> If, for example, the great majority of students, despite some appearances to the contrary, are not involved in political or social issues and do not expect to be in the future, it would seem that colleges, instead of being disturbed by occasional

vivid manifestations of student "activism," should ask themselves what they are doing to encourage students to assume responsibility in the realm of public affairs. The primary need is to wake students up, not slow them down.[11]

(d) The temporal constraints on intellectual behavior within a university are in general becoming worse. Although teaching loads at the better schools and in the higher ranks of the academic profession have dropped to what is in some cases a controversially low point, students are under greater pressure than ever to declare majors, pick areas of specialization, and direct their activities toward preparation for professionally oriented graduate work. In many cases students are now encouraged to take some graduate courses as undergraduates, and programs have been developed whereby a student can earn a master's degree along with his bachelor's degree at the end of four years, if he cuts down on "liberal" electives and adheres to a fairly rigid curriculum. These opportunities doubtless are of value to some students. All the same they reflect a concern that values training over education, and an interest in processing Ph.D.'s in response to national need that undervalues individual needs. Just as high-level training requires time, so too does the broader process of liberal education. In addition, it requires *unallocated* time; time for reflection and re-evaluation, for raising questions instead of seeking answers, for shopping around intellectually. Summer often provides students with such time. But more and more they are pressured to devote summers to hastening instead of enriching their educations, and often they spend summers in environments so far removed from intellectual pursuits that there is little stimulus for intellectual development.

Radical suggestion for the reduction of temporal constraints on students: Develop a plan whereby students can, perhaps in the middle of their college careers, spend a semester *in residence* in a viable intellectual community, with full time off from the normal academic requirements—in short, an undergraduate "sabbatical." Many students now take such a sabbatical, but do so at their own expense and without university sanction. They simply lose the time as far as progress toward their undergraduate degrees is

[11] "17 to 22: The Turbulent Years," *Stanford Today*, Jan. 1966, p. 9.

concerned. Still, their numbers increase, and their influence on some campuses is substantial. The suggestion calls for recognition of such a period as a legitimate and potentially highly beneficial part of an overall educational experience. The striking success of Harvard's highly selective Junior Fellows program suggests that the technique might have broader successful applicability. Why not grant one such sabbatical to any undergraduate in good standing who wants one? But continue his financial support, let him live on campus, and give him a full semester's credit toward his degree. Require absolutely nothing of him—but see that he is immersed in such an abundance of opportunities that he alone will set the limits of his accomplishments. Provide faculty members who will be available, at *his* option, for consultation and guidance. Welcome him in the laboratories and libraries, and in extracurricular activities and organizations. In substance, grant him full student rights, but without academic responsibilities.

Of course, some students will spend a semester futilely and fruitlessly, devoting the term to football or sex or hot rods. And there is admittedly one sense in which their degrees will mean a bit less than if they had been constrained by the usual requirements. But some of them, even after a term of frivolity, will return to the classroom with a new seriousness, maturity, and direction. And there will be some who will seize the opportunity with a vengeance; who will for the first time in their lives be able to devote themselves uninterruptedly to the pursuit of their own interests for a significant length of time. Many a physicist, physician, painter, and poet would be made during undergraduate sabbaticals. The problems of implementation, of course, are many. They could all be solved.

(e) The last suggestion leads naturally to consideration of the constraints imposed by lack of opportunity. The student on sabbatical, like his fellow students, will benefit most from the time he spends at the university if it provides, in addition to its classroom offerings, a viable community of active minds and the surroundings and activities on which they thrive. This means that the university should undertake active concern with the provision of a wide variety of cultural offerings, of inexpensive gathering places, and of an inviting and exciting bookstore. Cremin writes that "the way to nurture good taste is to make the good so widely available that the cheap ceases to satisfy." The university can undertake to make the good so available in the arts, in scientific activity, in the humanities, and in enlightened concern with social issues, that those within the university community will cease to be satisfied by what is cheap aesthetically, academically, or politically. The absence of such a surrounding places a constraint on the student's freedom to learn, and it is properly the university's business to combat this sort of constraint.

Throughout, I have argued in support of Searle's maximalist theory of freedom—the conviction that the university must minimize constraints of its own imposition and must in addition actively oppose many other kinds of constraints to whatever extent it can. There is, of course, no possibility that a universiy can provide a wholly free environment, disconnected and isolated from the pressures and values of society. But that is no misfortune. Proponents of the liberating university seek no ivory tower. Rather, the aim is to turn back to society the fruits of academic freedom, in the interests of a better social order in which freer individuals can thrive. Too many of our citizens have lost the child's sense of wonder and beauty that the sensitive and artistic adult retains. Too many have become so hardened that they do not even wince at the encroachment of creeping ugliness that has been a fruit of industrial and commercial progress and growth. They do not really see the slums or smell the foulness of urban air, or feel the horror of the threat of war. But among our youths, more frequent sparks of awareness appear, and occasionally burst into flame. Half our citizens are youths, most of whom have no say in the direction of social development and are getting rather little in the way of adequate education to prepare them for the time when they will have a say. To educate them to the task of responsible leadership of a free society, we must provide them as much freedom to learn as is possible. To learn responsibility, one must be free to be irresponsible at one's own expense. And he is not free who is constrained by lack of opportunity or by inhibition, any more than he who is constrained by ignorance. To combat all of these constraints together is one of the challenges that the university must face.

I

I

□　Essay: PAUL GOODMAN

It is proper that I should lead off this discussion, because the position I want to espouse is one pure extreme of the problem of freedom and order. It's the anarchist's position, which I happen to believe in, but it would have to be presented anyway, even if there were no person here who believed in it. Now, the anarchist's position on freedom and order is based on a simple psychological hypothesis. In any behavior, force and grace and discrimination can occur only when the organism is spontaneously initiating its behavior, by some intrinsic motivation; when it is, in Aristotle's sense, a soul, because the chief characteristic of the soul, for Aristotle, was that it was a self-moving form. The best behavior is that of a soul meeting an environment which is not so intractable but that in some way the organism can cope with it. The organism starts with its own initiation, its own intrinsic motivation, and it moves in an environment, containing the object of its desire or aversion, where in some way the organism can cope. When behavior is of this kind it will be most forceful and most graceful, and most intelligent—will show most discrimination. Obviously, in the conditions of life this is not always possible, but when it is not possible, the results are not as good, and it is at peril that we create situations where it is not possible.

For instance, suppose kids are playing on the street and they don't know anything about traffic, etc., and the three-year-old rushes out into the street in the path of the oncoming cars. This has happened with me as with every parent; and those times—

with regard to my three children—are the only times I have ever hit them, because obviously they have to learn to stay out of the way of those cars. Otherwise all problems would be ended; there would be no further initiation or coping or anything else. But the effect of this coercion is that the child now feels a little more uneasy on the street, has to watch his step; and, watching his step, there's a certain sense in which he's not going to run as headlong to the things which are important to him. Then there's less grace and force. Thus, in our city planning and in our education, I think we ought to try as much as possible not to add to the inevitable troubles of the world our own man-made, administration-imposed troubles.

It is for this reason that in my remarks on education in general, and I think it will be so today, I put a lot of emphasis on the early years, even though we are going to be discussing university administration, because the effect of the kind of mis-education that all of our children have gotten by the time they get up to the university is such that they in fact no longer know what they want; they have been too discouraged and too interrupted in their spontaneous learning. They don't trust their own best powers and instead they begin to introject, as we say in psychology; they begin to internalize and identify with external commands rather than with their inner motions and they think that that is how things must be. The result is that you can get college students who seriously discuss whether it is good for them to be graded; and they are obsessed at the age of twenty with grading. This would pass if they were eight, but one's a little ashamed of them—these grown people still worrying about such a thing. One can see only too clearly that after they get out of the university they're going to get jobs in which they will still worry about being graded, and if they're pleasing some standard of the boss's. At what point are they ever going to enterprise on their own, for the enterprise's own sake? This pattern obviously starts in our earliest years.

With this much introduction, let me turn to our subject, Freedom and Order. Now, in the popular wisdom it is thought that if you don't have imposed order you have chaos, as if spontaneous working out of impulse and coping with the environment did not have its own kind of order. But this is not the case; in fact, it's just the opposite of the case. Right order is nothing but the working out of free functioning. Take a simple example: when a tree grows, there's a very interesting mathematics where the branches occur—the phyllotaxis of leaves and branches—a very interesting mathematical law that is operating just because the growth impulse of the plant is meeting certain environmental conditions, conditions of gravity, osmosis, etc., which lead to a branching in a certain mathematical order; just as when a leaf forms it forms in a quite beautiful order or when a snail grows it has a certain beautiful order that is clearly not chaotic. Yet this is an order which is not imposed but is the result of spontaneous functioning, working itself out.

Let me take a rather more controversial case. In a recent study of animal psychology by Harrison Matthews, an English naturalist, he was struck by the fact that the animals in a zoo fight, often to the death, whereas in the wild the same animals do not fight at all. Why should that be? After long observation he thinks he has found the answer. The animals when young don't know their powers and they "play fight," as cubs or puppies "play fight" all the time. But in this process each one learns his territoriality. He learns just about what and how much of the environment he can really control, and how much the other one can really control, and how much must be conceded in respect to the other one, and the stronger animal also respects the territoriality of the weaker one. And, in the wild, where there is enough social space as well as geographical space, the animals learn to live together quite peacefully.

But in a zoo there isn't space for them to learn to grow up and so they never grow up. Meanwhile, their teeth have grown and their claws have grown, etc., and so this "play fighting" becomes extremely bloody, and of course once the animal is hurt, then the animal retaliates. So, Mr. Matthews says, the zoo is like a city—an overcrowded city—and his conclusion concerning urban overcrowding is that you cannot have decent life in the city. I think he's right, by the way. But here's an example of spontaneous growth in an interpersonal situation, where order emerges.

On the other hand, consider an imposed order, as for instance when we decide that all American youth ought to learn such and such and such, or all of them ought to be liberally educated and that a liberal education includes a survey course in mathematics and a survey course in American history, etc. Such order necessarily creates emptiness of function, and finally chaos. In the anarchist's phrase, "order" is chaos, just as property is theft. "Order" is chaos. The order of a policeman is chaos, because, in fact, it is preventing function, and therefore perversion of function begins to occur—feelings are repressed, behavior is inhibited. Explosion is inevitable. Resignation is inevitable. Such order is not harmony. The harmony that administrators impose is generally the "harmony of the graveyard." Whereas in a live conflict there's confidence—this is the democratic faith, isn't it?—that the truth will emerge. The error that the imposed order makes is to assume that administrators know the values beforehand. But they don't know the powers beforehand, which are concrete and usually individual; and they don't know the truth beforehand, which emerges only out of live conflict. Values emerge out of trying to function in the world. Now this process is often very hectic—very disorderly; of course it is. But there is no alternative. The notion that you can impose order from the outside only leads to chaos, and it certainly leads to loss of function, which is more important.

In our modern educational practice, there's a whole series of destructive impositions of this kind on the free growth of the growing human animal, and I would like to mention briefly about five of them, and then try to give what I think is the more correct method of obtaining freedom and order in education, including the university.

In the first place, there is an increasing extension of one tightly ordered system, one tightly scheduled educational process which goes from age three (e.g., the Head Start program) to maybe up to age twenty-two. That's a long time—twenty years! It is an imposed hierarchical order in which a youngster goes from grade to grade, by promotions and examination, and woe if he falls off the ladder—he can't get back on. It's a very tightly imposed order, and in fact, with upgraded curriculum and all that, it's being speeded up, so that the tensions of the upward climb get to be stronger and stronger. Further, on this upward ladder, it has gotten to be that the methods appropriate for small children have more and more tended to infiltrate and permeate the whole ladder. It's a kind of "schoolmarm" maternalism which might be not inappropriate for ages six and seven, but which is now practiced by most deans of students at the university level. They interfere with your hair-do and your social life and your free speech and political action, and whether you can drink, and then impose dormitory rules. These are methods used with quite small children. They teach by assigning lessons and talking. This method doesn't work for small children either but it's the schoolmarm method. So it's this extension of methods that are appropriate for children—or not even appropriate but at least traditional for children—that tends to hinder maturation in the high school and college years. It cuts down the possibility of the reappearance of initiative at adolescence, when it might be hoped for. The youngster continues to be treated as a child.

All of you who are in school now will admit, I think, that you've been disappointed that high school has been very like grade school, and college has turned out to be very like high school. I don't think that that was the idea of these educational institutions at the beginning. There were supposed to be sharp breaks. But there are not sharp breaks; and in fact the levels are becoming more and more homogeneous. I think anybody in the school business will admit that that's the case. Likewise, there's the attempt to impose on 100 per cent of the population, at least up to age eighteen, one establishment for growing up. The only environment in which the young are allowed to grow up is the school box, with its academic methods. This is a fantasy! In 1900 only 6 per cent graduated from high school, and yet the world went on, rather better in many respects than it does now; certainly not chaotically. There were then many channels for growing up, depending on choice, condition of life, luck. There were possibilities to go in and out of one channel into another channel; but now there is only one path, it's tightly graded, and re-entry is very difficult.

Consider the one method, the academic method—the school boxes with abstract curricula and textbooks, taught by specialist teachers who are specialists in teaching a textbook. This way of learning *is* fit for a certain number of characters, including many bright kids and many rather mediocre kids who belong in academic life. It's hard to know how many. Conant guesses that the academically talented are 15 per cent—well, let's say that's the figure. It's certainly nothing like 100 per cent. On the other hand, there are many kids who can only learn non-academically, if they're in real life for keeps, working on real jobs with something to show for it, and there are some who can only learn if they mull in their own way, and browse and brood, and don't follow graded courses. These are two types. Probably there are half a dozen well-marked types of learning. But no, we have one abstraction that we impose on all of them and call it education. That is, we make an abstract identification of education with going to school. The result is, I think, that for the most part, for most young people, *they learn nothing*, except what they can manage to learn during the periods of escape. They certainly don't learn in school. James Conant says that most kids in most high schools are academically there for about ten minutes a day, and all the rest is day dreaming, fiddling, home room. They're there in the body, but it doesn't mean a thing.

Likewise, there is a fatal tendency to use academic standards for professional licensing. The same people, the Board of Regents, who run the school system also decide who can be an architect. Therefore, if you decide to become an architect you have to go through the school system. It's inevitable that Regents will think that way. But for the Board of Regents to do licensing is a fantasy! They're the last ones who should do licensing because they will of course support their own establishment. They can't think in any other terms; and of course there is just plain imperialism, by which they aggrandize their own establishment. Yet academic degrees might be quite irrelevant. Take social work, for instance. A Master of Arts in social work is necessary in order to become a social worker to work in a settlement house in New York City, if the settlement house is going to get public money. But it's a fantasy! For this is not the way to learn to be a social worker. There's no reason why the worker should not come from some other framework, of philanthropy, the church, the housing project, etc. There are many things, like architecture, which cannot be taught in colleges. You teach architecture as an apprenticeship, in terms of real buildings being built in a master's office. That's the way those arts historically were taught and the only way that makes any sense. But now, sure enough, you have to have that degree from a university, and so on, to be an architect. There's no sense to it at all. But of course, naturally, anybody who's interested in architecture must go through the routine. Now it probably discourages a few who would be architects—it's hard to know how many good architects have been driven from the fields that way—but it does nothing for the practice of the good architect. We have been devoured by an abstraction. We begin to apply academic methods to the whole range of humane subjects, even though many of them are not academic in their essence at all. Here is an imposition of an arbitrary a priori order which can only create, I think, loss of function, or at least a tremendous waste of time.

Again, let us look at the schooling itself—the school system, the a priori scheduling, the extrinsic motivation provided by the grading system. All this is quite irrelevant to the concrete learning process of any kid. Because that's always individual with regard to the time when he's ready to pick something up and the style with which he's going to pick it up. And programmed learning is even worse. Take a programmed lesson, in geometry. Good geometricians have different styles. There are some who use algebraic methods really, to solve a geometry problem, and there are others who always make constructions—surrounding the problem with a kind of scaffolding in terms of which they get it into what they know, and then solving the problem. And others look at the problem intuitively, like music, and then suddenly see the relations emerge. These are different styles. But no! In programmed learning there's one way to get to that problem, to get to the answer. Now, if that particular way happens to fit your style, good; but if it doesn't, you are turned into a stupid ox. And I think, by and large, that it can be said that the school systems in this country as a whole are stupefying. For instance, in the state of California, the IQ in the high school is lower than in the public school over the state as a whole, and that's a middle-class state. I am not saying that the schools are the sole cause of children's becoming stupid but I think in California they probably are the chief cause.

In Harlem, on the other hand, we have several causes. In Harlem the IQ tends to drop ten points every three years of school going. That's a serious thing—a thirty-point drop in IQ over that nine years of school. In Harlem, it probably is the case that it's the combined effect of the home, the street, and the school that results in stupefaction. But it certainly is the case that when no attention is paid by the school to the time and style and language and class background of learning—nor to the environmental meaning, whether you're learning for real or whether you're learning as an apprentice or whether your learning fits your personal needs—that the vast number are going to be stupefied. And so it is.

A final way in which a priori abstractions create an arbitrary order and destroy freedom and function is the invasion of teaching and learning by criteria extrinsic to the whole province of education, such as national needs, going to school to get a union card, etc. In these cases, we substitute test-passing and role-playing for the performance of the learning task altogether. And yet, this is accepted as perfectly reasonable. The country, because of Sputnik, etc., needs such and such many engineers. Therefore, we're going to impose a kind of curriculum on 100 per cent of the kids, and weed out a certain number of algebraists. I doubt if you get the algebraists that way; you would have gotten them anyway. And meantime, what's happened to everybody else? In the end, we get a society which looks more and more educated in the sense that more and more have passed tests, and more and more have degrees, but in fact, in which no learning has occurred. I mean really none, literally none; except one very important kind of learning—how to avoid getting caught, how to get by.

Well, now let's talk about remedies. And first a remark about the university. My own feeling is that we ought to take the present university structure—at Western Reserve, certainly at the University of California—and just let it fall apart into its simple communities of professors, etc., who know something and are interested in teaching it, and students, who want to find out something. Or if the students don't know what they want, let them be allowed to shop around, with no sanctions, no penalties. Just let the whole fall apart and be reconstituted into its proper communities according to immediate functioning, and intrinsic motivation for all the people involved.

On the high school level, I would open a variety of ways of being educated for adolescents—academic ways; apprenticeship; technical training by corporations; self-study; subsidized programs of choice, like the GI Bill; and working in subsidized real cultural enterprises like local radio stations, newspapers, little theaters, etc., in order to provide a community service, but also, while doing that, to be scenes in which a certain number of adolescents can be educated by working. All these should be publicly supported. We ought to spend much more money on education than we do, but we ought not to spend one penny more of money for education by giving it to the present school administrators. I think we have already gone too far in that direction, far beyond what they are competent to handle or what they ought to have been given. We ought to spend much more money on education and try as much as we can to take away a good deal of what is now given to school people. Naturally, this is not the disposition of the Great Society.

Also, we have to open opportunity for leaving and re-entry of the academic system or apprentice system or any other system. We must open more possibility of crossing over and back. What's wrong with the European system is that they cut the non-academic off from the academic so sharply that there's no way to pass in and out again. Or, if you're apprenticed in one career, you are stuck with it; but there ought to be opportunity for several tries, as well as to return to the academic line. Return to college might depend on passing College Boards, without high schooling. But in fact serious research studies—the Eight Year Study—have proved that preparing for the College Boards is rather irrelevant to college performance. In the Eight Year Study the progressive schools that deviated most from preparing for college entrance produced kids who in college adjusted best. But nobody wants to listen to that study. That study, which was made in the thirties, is as if it did not exist. We do quite the opposite—we tighten the examining and force the preparation to be more and more narrow for the College Boards. But then we've also been taking the colleges and turning them into glorified high schools, so the theory is self-proving. If they do well in the high schools then they will do well in the colleges. It's self-proving because they're doing the same thing. Afterwards they get out and they get good salaries. And this is the final proof. Inevitably, since the licensing for the job has nothing to do with performance.

Again, although teaching and learning is a very complex ethical and psychological relation, sociologically it is extremely simple. All you need is a couple of teachers who know something and students who want to learn something. Therefore, I would drop all of the administrative superstructure entirely, admissions requirements and grading, etc., and restore all of these functions to the teacher-student relationship. If the teacher feels like teaching you, good, you're his pupil. If he doesn't want you, it doesn't make any difference what your credits are or your high school, or anything— you're out of luck. You find somebody who will teach you; in the end that's what it comes to anyway. If we reduce administration to janitoring and bookkeeping—which is all they really do—the educational communities could be immensely cheaper and probably smaller. Now I don't mean there shouldn't be a lot of young people and a lot of teachers in one geographical area. A large number is rather nice; it makes a little city. But the units of control should be small. Thirty thousand students may be congregated in one place, but there's absolutely no reason why the thirty thousand shouldn't be a hundred or two hundred educational communities, each self-administering. And I don't see that this would lead to chaos; on the contrary, it would lead to order. I would make each community entirely self-governing in all social matters. Curriculum is determined by what the teachers want to teach, because in the end that's all they're going to teach anyway. If they're made to teach what they don't want to teach, they teach it rigidly and badly, and in fact most teachers can't even be bullied into doing that. They *will* teach what they want to teach. You can assign me English 403 but I'm going to be teaching the next book I'm writing. That's in fact what it's going to be about. In my opinion, this professional freedom will sooner help the students find themselves, because they will be confronted with live intellects and if the intellect is relevant to them, good; they will stay with the teacher. If the intellect is irrelevant, they will realize the teacher is not for them and they will go some place else. There's no hoax that a student is getting a general survey which will expose him to something which he would otherwise never get. There's no evidence that any of this means anything; it's intensely inefficient.

Finally, I want to say something to the students. What the students must do is ask themselves with regard to these beautiful professions and arts and sciences that are around: What is the world I want to live in? What kind of community do I want? What is life about? What does this profession which I think I'm interested in add to that? What can it give to society, and to a good society? What skills and knowledge do I need to learn in order to play my part in that profession for that purpose? Having asked these questions, demand that that is what the teacher teach you. I think this would be desirable for the teacher, because it makes the teacher have to answer the demand, it makes the teacher have to prove the relevance of what he's teaching to the future society as well as the present society (or no society at all); and it also will return to our society what is entirely lacking at present, an infiltration into society of professional intellect. At present we have technically competent people but we don't have professionals who are posing the problems and criticizing the assumptions; instead we have a competent professional personnel who are solving the problems which have been stated by other groups. And this is just where the university is entirely failing. The only way to get the teachers back as a social force, I think, is for the students to demand that the teaching be relevant to a good society. I think these principles are quite sufficient to relate school to society.

I'd like to make just one last remark. The college years really ought to be a new beginning to the young people. I was at the University of Vermont a few years ago and a student pointed out at a public meeting that the university had entirely failed him, because when he came to the university he thought that it would shake his faith. He had heard that that is what happened when you went to college. But the university hadn't shaken his faith! And therefore in an important way the college was a total failure for him. He said he might as well have been in high school where they were afraid to shake his faith.

■ Reply: SANFORD H. KADISH

I trust Paul Goodman will not take offense at my agreeing with him—his was indeed an extreme statement. Let me respond to some of his intriguing and challenging observations in the order in which he made them.

I have some doubts about the relevance to the issue which we are confronted with of his original observation, about order being the working out of free functioning. In some kind of poetic metaphorical sense, I dare say there is something in that observation, if you're talking about the shape in which trees grow, which is a kind of "order" in response to functioning. But in terms of living in a community of individuals and of reconciling interests in order to provide for the maximum freedom for all, I don't know about this spontaneous working out. It seems to me that the Watts incident in Los Angeles was in some sense spontaneous, and it surely was a working out, but I would hardly think that that was anything less than the very chaos which Mr. Goodman suggests is produced by order and is negatived by free working out. I think the view of order which Mr. Goodman has is probably a different one than the one that I have. He seems to suggest that to justify order you have to attribute to the ordering authority some claim on its part to the truth—that they *know* what people should do, that they *know* what is right. I don't myself conceive of order in that way. When I graduated from law school and they gave us our diplomas after we accumulated a certain number of credits and passed a certain number of examinations, the dean addressed the students and talked about the wise restraints that make men free. Certainly there are kinds of restraints, of ordering principles, which don't rest at all upon a claim to truth, but which make it possible for the community to function—which make it possible to maximize the condition of freedom for the largest number of persons in the community. And order in this sense is not chaos, nor does it represent a claim to truth, but rather a commitment, that whatever truth is, it may be found by the freedom of persons to pursue it, in the kind of environment which makes that possible.

Then Mr. Goodman talked about the destructive impositions of the modern educational practices. I take it that he was making some very general criticism of aspects of modern education, and I hardly feel myself in a position to defend everything about modern education. I agree with a lot of what he said about modern education. For example, I would hardly take the position that it's desirable to use childish methods on adults, obviously. And, insofar as he is objecting to the excessive maternalism of university deans-of-women types, with respect to student behavior, all I can say is we have found a point of agreement. Concerning his point about the restriction of education to schools and the use of school methods, I think there is considerable validity to Mr. Goodman's very suggestive point. Perhaps we do tend too much to see the possibilities of education as being limited by the house Mr. Goodman talks about—the form of an organized university. Certainly it would be helpful if we engaged our attention to making more versatile the kinds of opportunities which we provide for various kinds of education.

He then talked about the attempt to treat academically the kinds of subjects which are not academic and ought not to be treated that way. The observation is really, to my mind, kind of a concretization of the first point about order, and he gave some examples. Now, some of these examples I don't agree with, and I want to mention them, not that in themselves they are so important, but because they suggest some essential differences between Mr. Goodman and myself.

Mr. Goodman talked about schools of social work—said they didn't really belong on campus; the best way for persons to get education in social work was to go to settlement houses. He talked about architects; schools of architecture don't belong on campus in the context of a university; the best way is to go out and apprentice yourself. And I suppose Mr. Goodman might also have said the same about lawyers and law schools, and it was very kind of him not to. Well, I think he's dead wrong. There's no general principle that can solve that one; it's merely an observation about what it means to be a first-class social worker, to be a first-class architect, to be a first-class lawyer—what the skills and the ambit of knowledge and insights and styles of being one of these things is. It turns on a judgment ultimately of how you ought to teach—apprenticeship versus a kind of academic discipline. Consistently enough, Mr. Goodman has little use for what is "academic" and for "discipline," and even less for "academic discipline."

First of all, there's lots of room in the house—the academic house—for a variety of instructional techniques. If I may use the law school as an example, insofar as we think the inclusion of bread-and-butter kinds of day-to-day realities of law practice can be helpful in molding the ultimate product, we try to bring that to students. And so we give them legal memos to write and we send them to institutions in the summer to work as interns in correctional institutions and in law offices. We have "moot" court programs, that is to say, legal arguments, with judges and with juries, and so on. But I would suggest that this is the proper way in which to improve the quality of education of specialists—to do it deliberatively, with controls, with careful thought about what kinds of things are important—to becoming a lawyer, a social worker—and to mold the educational environment in such a way as to make it most likely that we will achieve that goal. But to suggest, as Mr. Goodman does, that we just turn it over to a busy social worker; say, "Go work in a settlement house and see how your other settlement house workers are handling things"; or, I take it, send the young man to a law office—I think this is the abandonment of intelligence. We in the law used to do it that way; that's the way we used to educate lawyers until about sixty years ago. We just turned them over to law offices and they watched and the lawyers sent them on errands and they filed papers and occasionally they read a little bit, and then they learned how to manipulate the system. They became operators. But if you're interested in accomplishing anything more sophisticated, I suggest that the last thing you want to do is turn it over to the practicing profession, whether it be social workers, or architects, or lawyers.

I think one criticism Goodman made about modern education was overstated—the observation that university education responds far too much to extrinsic criteria of national needs. I suppose that in some measure it's true in engineering schools and sciences. But I don't think it's right with respect to other departments and colleges of the university. In instruction in philosophy, in economics, in political science, in the arts, in the law, in the bulk of the programs of general liberal education in the universities, I just don't think it's true. Nor do I find helpful Mr. Goodman's leftist cliché that a main, substantial problem of modern university education is that it is too much concerned with the preoccupation of the ruling group in American society.

Let me turn to his observation about letting the university fall apart, which particularly titillated, I take it, the student audience here tonight. It titillated me a little bit, too; it would be rather nice in some ways. One of the reasons suggested for letting the university fall apart was that it would encourage a kind of "reaching up" to its own level of each kind of activity. That would make possible a kind of federalization, a diversification so that you could have self-study and apprenticeship programs and technical working for corporations, and therefore that would be good. I have several observations to make about that. First, of all, I don't see why in order to achieve this diversification of the techniques of education, it is necessary to have the university fall apart—I don't see why it follows! I just don't see the connection. Secondly, it would seem to me that so far as the volume of administration is concerned, the administrative red tape, it may be that the program may have the opposite effect, because when you have people working in corporations in various places, and you have people working at home and taking trips to Europe, and then people going to school, you may have *increased* the need for paper work and co-ordination. I'm not sure the solution fits the problem.

His next observation had to do with the small-community approach to education. Goodman suggested first of all dropping admission standards, requirements, and grading, and so on. Well, as a professor of fifteen years' standing, who has suffered at least twice a year with the problems of grading hundreds of blue books, I am made warm and wistful by any such suggestion. I'm not sure, however, it's all that simple. About just letting the thing break down, without any need for administration, the fact is that at Berkeley we've got 27,500 bodies, young bodies! And a lot of old bodies, also. And they all work in the same place. It is a kind of city. It is a nice, utopian dream to have a city without rules where everybody goes his own way and free-functions his way through life and through everybody else—but, you know, I find it difficult to imagine how that's going to work out with 27,500 students at Berkeley. The administration does some useful things. And so far as I am concerned, the most useful thing they do is to look after things that otherwise I would have to worry about. You bet your life. Because I think that what I'm doing is important! Now there we have a point of basic disagreement, I dare say.

Let me take his observations about curriculum—teachers ought to teach what they want to teach. Well, they really do, you know. We *do* teach what we want to teach, pretty much, and I don't find the slightest inhibition from the administration with respect to my teaching what I want to teach. I do think there are limits, however; I don't know whether Mr. Goodman would agree, but there ought to be limits on what I can teach. If I undertake in the law school, for example, to teach a course in constitutional law, but at that moment, because I have a friend named John Searle, I happen to be interested in the theory of language and want to learn all about it, I don't think I should teach the theory of language, even though I was vitally interested. This is the notion of a kind of rough consensus on division of labor. I think that within that rough division of labor we've agreed upon, I am altogether in favor of the professor's finding his own way, talking about what interests him, rather than in accordance with some artificial imposition.

As for the point that we ought to meet the student needs, that that ought to be a principle for shaping the curriculum—absolutely. But who determines what the student needs are? I think Mr. Goodman begs the question. Everybody would agree we're trying to meet needs, but first of all is the problem of what a student need is. A student comes up to you and says, "I need a course in sitting-in in the South, because it's vital to *me* and that's what counts. I don't *care* about the theory of language and I don't *care* about social work. I don't care about anything but this problem of sitting-in in the South." Well, that may be. That, I think, is a relevant consideration in deciding what you want to teach—the psychological and moral and value position of the students you are teaching at a certain time. But the notion that we ought to cater to that need because *they* think it's the need I would reject outright. But, is that an issue? That they ought to demand? Is there any question that students are free to demand anything they like? I will no longer pursue that. My only point was that education ought not to be a catering to a student's apprehension of what his needs are. There is some affirmative obligation on the part of us, the professors, the specialists, to bring some constructive contribution to it. If the only point is that they ought to make themselves heard on what they believe they need and that we should listen and consider, then I'm in agreement. But I judge Mr. Goodman has in mind bigger game—student control of curriculum and course content—and here, of course, I am wagering my teaching career that he is quite wrong.

■ DISCUSSION

M. KADISH: If the discussion between Mr. Goodman and Mr. Kadish had gone on, very likely Mr. Metzger and Mr. Searle would have had no chance to say anything. This does seem to suggest the value of organization as a mediation between conflict. Spontaneous expression of energy in social contact may conflict, and we have to make choices. Therefore, we need an organization *for* the making of choices. Now I am not at all sure that Mr. Goodman will disagree with this. At any rate, it will start the ball rolling.

P. GOODMAN: I think this is a singularly unfortunate example for your point of view, because it might be then that Mr. Metzger, who was interested in our exchange, would have gotten involved, and I would certainly have learned a lot then from his live involvement. At a certain point he would have spoken up, because if he was interested he certainly would have had a point of view. It might then be that we would have wasted or used up all our time this afternoon, but then it could easily be, at least for the students here, that if there were a real live engagement of our minds with them becoming involved, it probably would have been just as well if next week their classes were called off and we went on. Isn't it possible that insofar as disorder has some creative aspects, you can't decide beforehand when it's going to happen? The spirit bloweth where it listeth. Now, if it can't blow in the universities and in the art galleries, where the devil can it blow? You're not going to have it blow with traffic scheduling, but it *might,* perhaps, occasionally ignite in the university halls.

M. KADISH: The spirit bloweth where it listeth, but so do airplane schedules intervene.

P. GOODMAN: This is just the problem that becomes the critique of our whole economy, where we're all rushing on from day to day and no wisdom occurs, and naturally we then rain bombs on the Vietnamese. Is this in fact what we want human life to be like? This more and more tightly regulated kind?

M. KADISH: I merely argued that this was an illustration of how, under certain circumstances, we have to make choices and we have to use patterns of decisions which are not simply spontaneous in terms of the interests of those who are involved at the moment. There are superordinate considerations. There's a need for civil society.

■

P. GOODMAN: On Mr. [Sanford] Kadish's remarks. I was rather thunderstruck that he chose the Watts incident as an example of spontaneous initiation. He knows, I am sure, better than I, having been down in that part of the world, that the Watts incident was precisely the result of repression of spontaneous forces, and the imposition of order. It was caused by the fact that they could not stand those cops who had brutalized them. It's a specific issue that came up again and again. Meanwhile, these people were living huddled together in a situation where they constantly had order imposed on them—an order which was imposed from outside and not spontaneously theirs; therefore, there got to be a "boiling up" of repressed energies and then the inevitable explosion. Watts is precisely an example of the incorrect relation of freedom and order, rather than the correct relationship. You see, what you're using as an example against my position is exactly the example I would have used against what's done in the ordinary course of society. Now when you speak of wise restraints making freedom, that *does* make for freedom, that's true, of course. We always come to arrangements when we're having conversation. I say my say and then after a while I can see that you want to answer, and I let you answer, and it goes on that way.

I think there's a presumption that there's a crowd named administrators, deans, etc., who are the wise inventors of wise restraints. I don't see why a small collection of students might not arrive at as many wise restraints as anybody else, especially if their skin is at stake. I myself, for instance, am an anarchist; I have a tremendous admiration for the common law. I think it's in a way the wisdom of all kinds of people in a whole range of cases and details which no single person or any group a any one time could possibly think of because it's too multifarious. But this whole collection of precedents and commentary on precedents, etc., over the years is a *remarkable* body of wisdom about human life. Well, what does that mean for an anarchist? That if somebody's committing a crime or something like that, we restrain him the way in an insane asylum you restrain the guy when he's banging his head against the wall and causing immediate damage. You calm things down. Then you take him to the judge and the judge says, "Young fellow, let me tell you what the common wisdom of the Anglo-Saxon people is—the law is such and such and such. Now, get out of here." Coercion only causes damage. Only. It never causes anything but harm. A certain kind of restraint until things calm down and listening to the wisdom, fine. But the notion that the wisdom belongs necessarily to administrators or people in power—that's a fantastic error we see belied every day. And you go into any court of law in New York at the lowest level—all you see is ignorance. You see some wisdom in the docks but you see only ignorance behind the bench! Even when the drunks are in there they generally have more sense than the magistrate. And certainly more human morality.

s. KADISH: To pick up just one small point on Watts, Mr. Goodman. I will hold my case. Watts *is* a good example of what I had in mind. On the Watts uprising I think no one would dispute me. It was spontaneous; it wasn't planned; it was unorganized. It was also a kind of "working out" in the sense that there were very important factors which contributed to it. It was a spontaneous working out. And yet I suggest to you that it represented anarchy, that it represented chaos, that it represented the destruction of order and not its nourishing.

You didn't refute that; your attack on the figure of speech is really an analogy. It is, "Well, look here; what caused Watts? Watts was caused by order." Nonsense! It was caused by a great combination of things. I think, from what I know, that what contributed to Watts among many other things was an unwise, unenlightened, foolish exercise of police authority by bigoted and small-minded and provincial police, led by a like-minded police chief. But to identify that with order is perfectly ridiculous —perfectly wrong! Why, of course, order can be abused; any authority may be abused. Authority may be badly exercised and it might be wisely exercised. Restraints might be stupid restraints or they can be wise restraints. But to say that there may be foolish restraints, to say that there may be abuses of authority, is *not* to make the case that all order must go. And therefore, I think that your assault on my analogy was not relevant.

■

W. METZGER: I should like to hear Mr. Goodman on this question: To dissolve large units, do you not need to construct other large units? For a long time, in this country, we dreamed of breaking up the trusts, of de-bureaucratizing the country. But a real structural change could only have been brought about by a powerful agency of government: say, an enormous anti-trust apparatus in the Justice Department. Also, to keep units small and the markets competitive, there would probably have had to have been a great supervisory apparatus—an FTC of enormous size. In short, when you try to change magnitudes, must not your instruments be in scale?

P. GOODMAN: I'd like to pursue the example because I think it will bring out the principle. In fact, what we have done is to aggrandize. For instance, we continually subsidize the big corporations; we decide that science research and development must be done through big corporations. It's pure superstition because the big corporations have produced a small fraction of any of the useful inventions and innovations of the last fifty years. But they are continually feeding at the public trough with all these subsidies because of this superstition they've created and that the public buys that they are indispensable. The best way of getting rid of big corporations is *not* to try to get rid of them directly but to set up countervailing forces, that is, to underwrite and subsidize the independents, the spontaneous, the local, etc. For instance, in TV, the way to get rid of the present hegemony of NBC, CBS, and ABC is not by breaking them but by making sure that the new UHF channels are given out to real independents with a rule against their joining a network! And insisting that if they confederate it be on another principle, not on a network principle. You see, that's the way I would get rid of it. I would do the same thing with regard to the monopoly in the press at present. I would put endless public money into underwriting small newspapers and give them a show on the market! In other words, I'd use Galbraith's principle of countervailence.

■

J. SEARLE: I've heard you speak on this line a lot, and I've always felt great about it and then I'd walk out of the room and forget it. Now, I'm trying to take seriously what it would really mean if the chancellor of the University of California went in Monday morning and did as you suggest—said to his staff, "Fall apart!" Because this is what you recommended—that the administration ought, in your words, to "fall apart." I'm trying to figure out what it would be like if we did that, if we took off and went fishing or went back to our departments or something like that; and it seems to me there's one function that we perform that's not performed by janitors and bookkeepers that I don't know how you intend to have performed, and that is, conflict resolution. That's really mostly what I do for the university. Resolve all sorts of very powerful conflicts, and not just within the university. A great deal of my time is taken up with a guy named

"Irate Citizen," and he's in there in the office and he's on the phone and he's writing letters, and if I don't do this or someone in the office isn't doing it, he's going to be bugging the professors—he's going to be onto the faculty. Similarly, there are all sorts of competing interests within the students, within the student political groups, fighting over the limited resources we have; and within the departments, fighting over the limited financial resources of the university. The primary function which the university administration performs is conflict resolution. It doesn't resolve them entirely on abstract principles; it resolves them with all sorts of mediation, *ad hoc* devices; you try to get people to compromise to a certain extent within the university. This is what Kerr describes. Now how do you want us to do it?

P. GOODMAN: My own feeling is that there are two kinds of conflicts; there are those conflicts which come from trying to keep together those things which do not naturally fall together in the same sphere, so that a fantastic amount of energy, including a lot of conflict resolution, has to be spent on the cement. So if you'd let the thing fall apart there'd be less fighting. Secondly, there's another kind of conflict which is real conflict, and real conflict should not be resolved. It should be allowed to solve itself creatively; it precisely should not be solved from outside; it should fight itself out, in an atmosphere of respect, the meaning of respect being that the people keep in conflict and don't end the conflict either by a violent blow or by leaving. That has to be done in terms of the general spirit and can't be done by administrators who tend *never* to create that kind of spirit. The chief reason you have all these conflicts at Berkeley is precisely the "keeping together" of parts which don't cohere!

J. SEARLE: I must confess I find that so abstract as not really to be much help in dealing with actual situations. I don't know what the cement is and what the glue is now. We've got all these departments, say, and as an example, we've only got a limited amount of funds, and the Physics Department wants to hire more professors and the Philosophy Department *really* wants to hire more professors. And now, I know exactly how this conflict would be resolved if it would be up to the Philosophy Department, and I know if you say, "Well, look, let things fall apart or just let the conflict go," I just don't know what that means. How do we deal with day-to-day problems on that basis?

P. GOODMAN: If it fell apart in fact, you would find that there were some philosophers who were really interested in a community of scholars who would ally themselves with some physicists who were interested in the community of scholars. The whole departmental system is precisely the result of keeping things together that don't belong together! The departmental system isn't even a university system! The result is a bad mix-up.

S. KADISH: I wonder on what basis you feel so confident in your belief that if a place like the university were simply to let itself fall apart, all these lovely consequences would follow. I mean, what kind of hard data do you have, what kind of evidence? What kind of argument except your very attractive, idealized commitment to the absence of order? I think that the very fact that it has been the pattern that some kind of coherent organization, a pattern of rules, a pattern of order, has been the predominant, unfailing pattern which has characterized social institutions throughout history is some evidence that there is something in the subject matter which demands it. I'm not suggesting that I've proven my case but I'm suggesting that I've established a prima-facie case for some kind of order, whereas all that you've asserted is a dogmatic absolute.

P. GOODMAN: At the time of Adam Smith there was a dogmatically imposed economy in England called mercantilism. And then this was allowed to fall apart into its natural functions which were joint stock companies without patents royal and monopolies—whereupon we zoomed into a period of tremendous production, called the modern capitalist system. And so human monopolies naturally formed. It is by no means the case that there's been an undeviating pattern of imposed crackdown order. Do you think the Bill of Rights in the American Constitution wasn't a sign of the introduction of a different kind of order? It is an order which was founded on the notion that if we let individual citizens operate, then democracy will flourish and the truth will emerge. This is a different kind of pattern. I don't mean pattern against no pattern. I mean an imposed pattern as against a functioning pattern. That's different.

■

L. CROCKER: Ideally order *should* be freely generated. Now it all depends on the meaning of the word "freely." I think there is no instance, that I know of, of a social order arising outside of a natural hierarchy such as the family relationship or a student-teacher relationship without dominant leadership on the part of those functionally equipped to lead. The notion of equality applied to unequals is fallacious and harmful. Mr. Goodman made a false comparison between biological order and cultural order. Does he want us, like the primitivists, to go back to a natural order—to the haphazard, the unguided, divorced from experience? His phrase—"the spontaneous working out"—seems to mean that. Mr. Goodman has exaggerated the despotism which he takes to be reigning in our universities just as he has exaggerated our treatment of students as children. There is some of that remaining, but less and less. Essentially we treat students as learners. Everything has its place; its place is determined by function. Shall we treat adolescents like adults? Shall we give learners equal status with teachers? It goes without saying that functions and places evolve and we must help them evolve—not impede them and not propose a philosophy of status quo.

The character of Mr. Goodman's thinking has obviously a strong messianic and utopian tinge. He would deliver us from evil into the promised land. I have a strong aversion to utopian thinking because it is inclined to absolutes, as we saw throughout his remarks, and ignores the unpleasant human realities or purports to escape from them. No utopias have ever succeeded and none ever will. Typical of utopianism is to think that complexities of modern institutions can be swept away and that we can return to a simpler form of life. We have only to abolish history, which is only a long error, and start again *de nouveau* with the stroke of a pen, armed with a rational plan!

It reminds me of Lord Keynes's criticism of Bertrand Russell. Russell, Keynes said, argues that all of our troubles are due to the fact that men have not lived rationally; therefore the remedy is to start living rationally.

Even if we had Mr. Goodman's anarchy, I think that new structures and rigidities would very soon arise by the nature of things, and these would become in turn the object of his criticism exactly like the present ones. He would have everyone learn at his own rate and in his own way. In *his* utopia teachers would teach what they want, but students would also study what *they* want. They might never meet! He wants the university detached from the society in which it functions and therefore drained of significance, prone to desiccation and futility. He ignores the fact he cites, that most students go to college not because of love of learning but because conditions in our society make it necessary for them to go. Finally, on the matter of deans, I am perfectly willing to accept the proposal that all deans should be abolished. I would exult in that, perhaps. However, I'm only afraid that something else will come up to take their place with a different name, because once again communities need and have the habit of finding modes of organization.

P. GOODMAN: There's only one word I want to say against that. I am all for organization. The question is, is the organization one imposed extrinsically on the functioning, or is it one which develops *from* the functioning? I'm not for disorder.

L. CROCKER: I happen to think that the modes of organization that we have, *have* developed exactly as you say; they may not be functioning that way anymore.

P. GOODMAN: That's right; I think many of them *have* developed that way, such as the free-market mechanism—an anarchist mechanism which developed extremely elaborate rules of organization. But then into it crept monopoly, which prevented the free-market organization, and then we have to regulate it. And one of the ways of regulating it is to break up the monopolies.

■

One last thing on natural depravity. I don't know how anything I have ever said gives anybody the impression that I'm a Rousseauian and that I think that man is good by nature. I'm an Aristotelian. I don't think man is either good or bad by nature; I think, in fact, what we mean by good is what it's human to be. And that the problem is how to fulfill the humanity of people, that is, the institutions of people which take the potentially moral animal and turn its morality one way or another way. I want to get rid of authority because since people might be evil, you do not give them power; and since power corrupts, we find that deans come on like deans and presidents have swelled heads, and they cause damage with the best will in the world. I believe with Aristotle that the reason why democracy is the good form of government is that it is the weakest—it is the chief safeguard against tyranny. If you allow people to have power they will abuse it. Therefore, I'm against authority. Don't you see, it's not because I think man is naturally good; it's because I think that man has too much of a disposition to become evil—quite the opposite of what these critics seem to think.

I. LEVI: I want to ask a question of Paul Goodman. How do you tell what *is* the proper functioning of any institution?

P. GOODMAN: You can teach a dog to walk on its hind legs and balance a ball, and it does it with certain behavioral characteristics. And you can take, for instance, a teaching machine and teach a child to perform in the same way. But a dog's action in the field when it's chasing a rabbit has, let us say, a grace and a force and a kind of discrimination and power of movement and a *Gestalt*, which is quite different from a dog's walking on his hind legs and balancing a ball. Now, in this case we have two rather clear-cut extremes and most people would say, "Yes, this is good for dogs," and there won't be any difficulty in saying in this case, "This is a dog coping with his environment according to its spontaneous impulses and its intrinsic desires." Observe the pattern of life at present! All you have to do is go to an elementary school the way I have done as a school board member who sat there hour after hour every week, and see these kids with glazed eyes being tormented or their youth wasted, and you cannot deny that this is evil, that it in some way doesn't fit them! That's all I'm saying; and if you say that you can't tell the difference, then I don't believe you!

II

Essay: Walter P. Metzger

Reply: John R. Searle

Discussion

II

◻ Essay: WALTER P. METZGER

In 1961, the federal courts, in two decisions, informed the administrators of state colleges and universities that the way in which they disciplined students, and to some extent their grounds for doing so, had to conform to the due process requirement of the Fourteenth Amendment to the Constitution. In the case of *Dixon* v. *Alabama State Board of Education*,[1] Judge Rives declared, in dicta, that students accused of misconduct had the right to these procedural protections: timely notice, specific charges, a hearing that is "something more than an informal interview," disclosure of the names and testimony of adverse witnesses, the right to call witnesses in their own behalf. In the case of *Knight* v. *State Board of Education*,[2] Judge Miller annulled a regulation making conviction of a criminal offense, regardless of its character, grounds for the summary expulsion of any student in a state-supported institution. The act that merits dismissal, Judge Miller said, is that which reflects "dishonor and discredit upon the institution in which [the student] is enrolled and upon higher education in general," and not simply and without probing that which violates the law.

The precedents from which these decisions departed were considerable. Heretofore, despite judicial warnings against arbitrariness, the courts had been lenient about procedures, either because they held, as in *Gott* v. *Berea College*,[3] that a college performed

[1] 294 F. 2nd 150 (1961).
[2] 200 F. Supp. 174 (1961).
[3] 156 Ky. 376 (1913).

59

parental functions and could therefore exercise parental powers, or because they held, as in *Anthony* v. *Syracuse University*,[4] that admission to a college was a privilege which the student accepted on the giver's express or implicit terms. Even less were the courts inclined to question the legality of grounds for dismissal. Recognizing the diverse types and environments of institutions, the courts had sanctioned the removal of students for such diverse offenses as smoking a cigarette in public, serving liquor at a party, attending a family celebration without permission, marrying in a civil rather than religious ceremony, passing a letter to a classmate asking to make her acquaintance, being a member of a secret society, preaching atheism, and—in the *Anthony* case just mentioned—not being "a typical Syracuse girl"!

I shall have more to say about the legal significance of these cases, but at the moment I wish to use them as a springboard to a discussion of the academic guild. From all apparent indications, the academic profession was not deeply interested in the issues raised by *Knight* and *Dixon*. Its journals did not notice them while they were *sub judice;* the American Association of University Professors, its major spokesman, did not submit *amicus* briefs. Though the decisions did arouse some excitement, especially among constitutional lawyers and the proctoral forces of academe, they did not have an immediate impact on the profession as a whole. The judicial rebuke to administrators, rendered on behalf of students, was a blow to autocratic academic government; but it caused little revelry in circles where the same reproof, in behalf of teachers, would have evoked an exuberant response. This inattentiveness (indifference may be too strong a word) is not inexplicable: the academic profession in America has long assumed that academic freedom and its attendant safeguards are the property of teachers, not of students; and it has consequently failed, except on such border issues as loyalty oaths, speaker bans, and disclaimers, to make the cause of student rights its own.

Professors do not usually state this matter bluntly, and some of them bristled when Sidney Hook, not one to waste words on equivocation, did so in a recent article in the *New York Times*.[5]

---

[4] 224 App. Div. 487, 231 N.Y.S. 796 (4th Dept. 1928).
[5] "Freedom to Learn but Not Freedom to Riot," *New York Times Magazine,* January 3, 1965.

Taking issue with the demands of some of the Berkeley partisans, Professor Hook declared that the American college student is entitled to two kinds of freedom only: that of the learner and that of the citizen. As a learner, he is entitled to be instructed by free professors; as a citizen, he is entitled to say and do what the law allows. The first freedom is passive and derivative; the second freedom, while active and personal, merely constitutes a shield against the state. But the person in *status pupillari*, according to Professor Hook, is not entitled to immunities of speech and action against sanctions imposed by the institution—which is what academic freedom largely means. Such immunities, he maintained, are designed to protect the transmission and advance of knowledge and are thus reserved for those who have gnostic competence, as certified by their appointments and tenure status. Students may, as a matter of enlightened pedagogy, be left to certain of their own devices (Hook himself was inclined to be quite permissive), but without that certifying *quid*, students can claim no prerogatival *quo*, and the same benevolence that releases them may, when it deems it necessary, rein them in.

As a reflection of the guild exclusivism that has long prevailed in academe, this pronouncement in my view is unexceptionable. But as a survey of the possibilities, it is parochial; as a definition of the principle, it is deficient; and as a professional precept, it goes astray. The divorce between academic freedom and student freedom is not a universal phenomenon; Hook generalizes from the American special case. The purpose of academic freedom in this country is not solely to protect expertness; Hook oversimplifies a complex claim. And the academic enterprise is not ennobled because professors get rights and students charity; Hook ignores the costs of discrimination. All of which suggests that Hook, like many of his less outspoken fellow guildsmen, has converted the idea of academic freedom into a professional ideology.

■

To show that the Hook statement is parochial, one need only compare it with the classical German view. Since the German universities in the nineteenth century contributed greatly to the rebirth of our own, and since the German concept of academic freedom was once widely commended on these shores, this is not an unduly stretched comparison, but one that measures our defection from a prime example and a borrowed norm.

To the Germans, *Freiheit der Wissenschaft*—their most inclusive term for academic freedom—had three distinctive but closely related meanings. It referred, first of all, to the right of the professor, as a civil servant, to be free from the ordinary disciplines of that service: to teach without adhering to an imposed curriculum, to publish scholarly and scientific findings without submitting them to an official censor, to shape—within broad limits—his own routines of work. Called *Lehrfreiheit*, these privileges were cherished by professors not only as adjuncts to free inquiry, but as symbols of the social deference paid to scholarship and to academic scholars as a class. But *Lernfreiheit*, or student freedom, was also part of the definition and also highly valued by professors. Literally, it meant "learning freedom," but it was more than a looking-glass prerogative—the right of a student to give attention to a teacher free to speak his mind. It was in effect a disclaimer by the institution of any authority over the student save that of qualifying him for degrees. This restraint was justified by and mirrored in a number of institutional arrangements. Free to move from university to university, sampling courses and professors, the German student did not bind himself to an institution in an exclusive way; free to absent himself from classes and exempt from all but ultimate examinations, the German student did not furnish an institution with repeated proofs of his proficiency; above all, forced to find his own lodgings and diversions, the German student did not submit himself to any institution as a tenant or a customer or a ward. In Germany, *Lehrfreiheit* and *Lernfreiheit* were presumed to be complementary: the mobility and self-reliance of the students to reduce the dangers of unfettered teaching; the flexibility and self-direction of the faculty to implement the students' right of choice. The third meaning of *Freiheit der Wissenschaft*—the dissociation of the university from the other branches of public administration—tightened the links between the other two. By the middle of the nineteenth century, the German university had regained the right to manage its internal affairs directly, though important financial and other powers were retained by the state ministers of education. This partial return to medieval corporatism enhanced the authority of the senior faculty, who, like the guild masters of old, elected university officials, framed educational policies, awarded the *venia legendi* to deserving neophytes, and exercised a limited power of co-option. Faculty control came to be regarded as a necessary corollary of *Lehrfreiheit*. But it was also understood to depend, as a practical matter, on *Lernfreiheit*—on the absence of guardian duties that would have required an elaborate administrative apparatus, invited supervisory intrusions by the state, and overtaxed the energy of the learned guild.

Americans trooped to the German universities in the nineteenth century not only to learn more about academic subjects, but to learn more about academic institutions. When they returned, many of them seemed as much impressed with the German concept of student freedom as with the German concept of professor freedom or the German mystique of research. Gradually, however, as they built indigenous universities, ostensibly under German inspiration, they modified and then abandoned the essence of the principle of *Lernfreiheit*. In 1885, when Andrew Fleming West wrote an article asking, "What is Academic Freedom?" he replied: non-compulsory chapel and elective courses— two concessions to student choice but a far cry from the full abnegative principle. In 1889, when Albion Small wrote an article entitled "Academic Freedom," he omitted all reference to students and concentrated on the problems of professors. In 1915, this conceptual break became canonical when it appeared in the Statement of Principles of the newly founded American Association of University Professors. The most elaborate analysis of academic freedom up to that time, the statement took cognizance of the fact that in Germany the term referred to both the teacher and the student. But, said the new voice of the academic profession, "It need scarcely be pointed out that the freedom which is the subject of this report is [exclusively] that of the teacher." Thus truncated axiomatically, the freedom that the association fought for was to remain exclusively that of the teacher: never, in all its subsequent history, was it to investigate or officially censure an invasion of the freedoms of the other class.

What caused this radical separation? Many who have asked this question have been inclined to look to our pedagogic ethos and stress its puritanic source. We were mistrustful of student freedom, Henry S. Commager and E. G. Williamson have suggested, because the doctrine of natural depravity, implanted in the early colleges, was never thoroughly uprooted, and because the doctrine of *in loco parentis*, adopted when undergrads were babes, remained lodged in our laws and expectations long after collegians came of age. Doubtless some importance should be assigned to the Calvinism in our culture and the lingering hold of parental norms. But these are not, it seems to me, the keys to the fate of student freedom. For one thing, youth was also catered to in this country, and the view that it should assume responsibility was at least in dialectic tension with the view that it should be closely watched. For another thing, given our educational diversity, the demand for a collegiate home away from home might well have been met, not in a total way, but by the setting up of special anchorages for the sons—and especially the daughters—of parents loathe to set them free. Moreover, the college *in loco parentis* was not a college acting on a proxy: its power to expel its students actually exceeded that of authentic parents, who would have been subject to criminal prosecution if they had cast their children out. Finally, it is difficult to see why the authors of the A.A.U.P. report, who were professors filled with research ambitions, should have wished to perpetuate older vigilances, or why, as late as 1915, when John Dewey was successfully mounting his assault on adult authority in education, an archaically strict philosophy should have retained so firm a grip.

I would put the explanatory emphasis on a different set of historic factors: the expansion of the college residential plant, the rise in faculty aspirations, and the break in faculty-student ties, as a result of their cultural estrangement. As I see it, these factors took effect, not in the distant past, but in the period of university construction—roughly from 1870 to the First World War; and their effect was not so much to rebut as unwittingly to undermine the rationale for student freedom.

Despite their reference to German blueprints, Americans did not build separate graduate institutions, but added them to a preexistent or specially constructed college base. One result was the intermingling of different student bodies; another—which I would stress—was the retention of the English residential system and its adaptation to more sumptuous surroundings. Starting from scratch, the wealthy University of Chicago assigned half of its building space to dormitories, the other half to lecture halls and laboratories. In the course of extensive renovations, older Harvard and Yale also built upward and across, erecting new abodes for students along with new abodes for science. In time, fed by growing endowments, the insatiable desire to quandrangulate had the effect of creating campus cities, whose activities were about as manifold as those of urban life itself. With great numbers living in its boarding houses, playing on its recreation fields, eating in its restaurants, recuperating in its infirmaries, the American university was to the German university what a metropolis is to a museum.

It can be argued that the more complex American form was more attuned to the learning process and more generous in its response to student needs. Be this as it may, it cannot be doubted that the greater encapsulation of the student by his university subjected him to more restraints. Inevitably, a *pension* requires a *concierge*. In theory, perhaps, it may be possible to regulate the use of an immense facility without over-regulating the users of it. In practice, that possibility is remote, especially when the regulators are themselves to a large extent unruled. One can imagine, for example, what would happen if the commercial owners of an expensive property, dependent for future rents and capital on its reputable use and punctilious upkeep, acting within the latitude of a charter instead of within the confines of a lease, were to lay down rules for youthful tenants whose admission had been granted as a favor and whose term of occupancy was short. To complete the analogy with the landlords of academe, one need only add in the latter's case a strain toward justice in evictions stemming from benign intentions and a cautiousness based upon the knowledge that current residents were future alumni and potential donors. Something more than a cultural lag was responsible for the parietal rules that characterized American universities. Behind the curfews and floor surveillances, the no-trespass signs and off-limits ordinances, the tense and unceasing patrol of the grounds and plant, lay not only a tradition carried over, but a new managerial solicitude stimulated by the heavy investment in the material side of student life.

To have survived in this opulently hostile setting, the principle of student freedom would have needed many professorial defenders. That few came forth can be attributed to a second factor: the preoccupation of the profession with its own sharply rising discontents. Unlike their counterparts in Germany, American professors were not the privileged servants of the state or the effective administrators of their institutions; they were the employees of lay governing boards and the subordinates of the latter's appointed deputies. This system of academic control, though it had had two centuries in which to grow conventional and had in that time grown more rational and more lenient, came to seem inordinately oppressive to many academics in the building age. In part, new roles inspired new resentments: now perceiving themselves as scientists and public experts, many professors chafed at an arrangement that had been formed when they were schoolmasters and little else. In addition, as the universities grew larger, they became more bureaucratic and impersonal, and the old discrepancies of power could no longer be allayed by communal intimacy. By the turn of the century, this blossoming sense of class importance and this weakening hold of irenic customs gave rise to an academic movement that sought to procure for professors a greater freedom from the dictates of administrators and a stronger voice in institutional affairs.

Since students had come under the same hegemony (this was the period when student counseling and student discipline fell largely into the hands of administrators), it might be supposed that the professors' movement would have embraced this *tertium quid*. But common subordinations did not result in a common cause. Professors found it difficult enough, in a pre–Elton Mayo environment, to persuade the managers of the university to share a substantial portion of their powers. To have waged two battles against the established system, one on behalf of a yet lower order, would have greatly magnified their difficulties while reducing their chances of success. Furthermore, to secure power in and freedom from the institution, professors found it necessary to proclaim their extra-institutional responsibilities: their roles as agents for their disciplines, their roles as counselors to public agencies. Characteristically, it was the administrator who reminded professors of their teaching duties and their roles as exemplars to college students; for here, where the interest of the institution was unquestioned, the legitimacy of his own authority was assured. There thus arose a triangular play of forces that can be observed in other kinds of institutions, including hospitals and welfare agencies: the professional divorcing himself from the client to enhance his own prestige and power; the administrator invoking the client's interest to keep the professional in line.

The educational literature of this period bears witness to a third cause of separation: a decline in the intellectual quality of undergraduates. Of course, one must take what professors say about their charges with a dose of skepticism; otherwise, one might be driven to conclude, from reports given out since the days of Mather, that the student mind was wretched at the beginning and has steadily deteriorated ever since. Still, the laments of the Wilsons and Canbys and other academic critics of the building age do seem, if not entirely unexaggerated, at least compatible with a number of academic facts. This was the time when American college students, though congregating in ever larger numbers, were still drawn from a privileged band of society; when American graduate students, though a growing part of the student community, were still too few to provide an offset to its callowness; when the American baccalaureate degree, owing to the vocationalizing of the curriculum and the widespread adoption of the elective system, ceased to testify to fixed accomplishments; when the American occupational structure, though growing increasingly specialized, did not yet call for academic virtuosity or much training beyond the four-year stint. For these and other reasons, this was the time when American campus life began to institutionalize its puerilities: when the football psychosis gained ascendency in places nominally devoted to the healthy mind; when the Greek-letter fraternities waxed palatial on the strength of their snobbery and prank appeal; when good form dictated mediocrity and the goal of student-gentlemen sank to "C." That this was also the time when professors were investing themselves in research, and evolving new and close relations between knowledge and the problem-laden world, points to the emergence of two cultures that had grown up in proximity but were out of touch.

Where the cultural gap was widest—in the largest, most secular, and usually most patrician institutions—it tended to foreclose alliances: professors were not easily persuaded that their hedonistic students suffered gross privations; students felt no immense compassion for professors unhappy with their lot. Sometimes, crisis dramatized this estrangement. In the two decades prior to the First World War, when attacks on the economic heterodoxy of professors produced great cases, famed victims, and heroic myths, the undergraduates were not often conspicuous in defending freedom, while the quondam students—the alumni—were often prominent on the attacking side. Of course, some professors were reluctant to implicate students in their own predicaments. But it would seem that the use of students as accomplices was as much enjoined by the cultural bifurcation as by any professional taboo. With their rituals of academic patriotism, their class suspicion of dissent, their alienation from the world of intellect, students were likely to make loyalty to Alma Mater stand for obedience to those officially in charge. In their time of trouble, professors turned to their own protective agencies—first to their specialist societies, then to the ecumenical A.A.U.P. Fighting their battles alone, they came more firmly to believe that theirs was a lonely battle, and that the privilege of academic freedom belonged solely to them by the right of war.

I would thus attribute separation to a set of accidents, occurring in comparatively recent times. But fortuitous causes can have iron consequences. The momentum of history can outstrip alternatives. The next question therefore becomes: Is it possible to rejoin what the past has sundered? In my view, it is entirely possible to extend academic freedom to students, even under American conditions. This is not to say that it can be extended to them in full, or precisely in the German manner. In America, academic freedom embraces five distinctive privileges: classroom autonomy for the teacher, freedom of inquiry for the scholar, extramural freedom for the staff member, tenure protection for the qualified, academic due process for the accused. Some of these privileges necessarily go with the professorial station—and it was to these that Professor

Hook referred. But some are not in fact status-linked, and the case for pre-emption collapses when they too are entered on the list.

Briefly to consider all five elements: In America, the academic teacher claims the right to control the podium of the classroom, to judge the performance of his students, to speak his own thoughts and not another's—to create, in short, a propaedeutic sanctuary, largely if not entirely under his own command. Plainly, it would undermine the privilege to yield it, though there may be room within its boundaries for consultation with students about curricula and even schemes whereby the judges may be judged. Perhaps it is fear of students' editing the grade book and jabbering from the well (a fear that can borrow validity from certain Latin American examples) that makes the guild so possessive about its privileges. But it had never been thought in Germany—surely the most apposite example—that students were free to usurp their masters, and it is even less likely in America, where students are under a much stricter classroom regimen, that the teacher-tester-checker can be displaced. The possibilities for extension lie not in the formal, but in the informal provinces of education. In our commodious universities, there are many learning arenas where grades and quizzes are irrelevant, where instruction is entirely self-inspired, where teacher prerogatives are not involved and cannot be threatened. Teacher autonomy in the classroom may thus find its proper American analogue in student autonomy in the library and auditorium—in his right to call in any speaker, to organize any club or forum, to read whatever book. This much *Lernfreiheit* in the lymphatic system to match that much *Lehrfreiheit* in the circulatory system gives the university an organic quality which a radical separation tends to destroy.

Secondly, the American professor asserts the right not to have to account to his institution for the contents of his scholarly and scientific work. Superficially, this component of academic freedom, since it refers to freedom of publication, may seem applicable to a specific student enterprise—the uniquely American campus press. But academic scholarship and student journalism are too different, operationally and functionally, to be joined under one embracive right. The academic scholar is accountable to fellow specialists who will evaluate what he publishes; the student journalist does not customarily submit to any external discipline. The purpose of academic inquiry is to extend the boundaries of knowledge; the purpose of student journalism is not everywhere a heuristic one. In some places, the campus newspaper is a laboratory of instruction and may be as much in need of monitoring as a classroom. In other places, it is a reflector of student sentiment and may be as much in need of regulation as an election center. Where it is primarily an academic detective—and increasingly it has taken on the function of exposing the secrets of the university and telling its members what is going on—it does discover and distribute knowledge. But in such cases, it may well deserve to be under wider auspices, for there is no reason why students should monopolize this necessary, difficult, and often mishandled task. Because tight controls would be self-defeating and prior restraint pedagogically unwise, the student press should be treated gently by that grace which Professor Hook describes. But this puts it in a different category from free inquiry, which must be unqualified and inviolable. In short, not every resemblance is an equivalence, and care must be taken, when tracing neglected parallels, not to rush into false analogies.

But nothing in fact or sound philosophy can justify the hoarding of a third prerogative: the right of a staff member, as a citizen, not to be punished by his institution for opinions uttered beyond the walls. Extramural freedom—the distinctively American contribution to the theory of academic freedom—owes little to the expertise of professors, since it is presumed to affranchise them on issues not specifically related to their specialties. Nor does it stem from the quasi-license of an appointment, which attests to scholarly competence, not political wisdom or polemic skill. It rests, instead, on the understanding that, in a society where civil liberty is a legally protected value and civic participation a widely acknowledged virtue, a university that disparaged either would demean its members and itself. A second-class civil status would not prove attractive to first-class intellects; a ban on speech outside a discipline (given the vague peripheries of knowledge) would have an inhibitory effect on speech within. Thus backed by the normative culture, the competitive urgencies of recruitment, and the general inutility of zonal ordinances, the privilege of extramural freedom cannot be said to apply to teachers and not to students, to the smaller and not the larger segment of the affected academic whole. It is interesting to note in this connection that Professor Hook ignored this third component, but limited his discussion to freedom of teaching and research.[6]

Academic tenure and due process are designed to protect the aforementioned freedoms. The operative meaning of tenure is that the holder, having demonstrated his ability, may not be removed from his position save for some serious dereliction proved in an intramural setting; the principle purpose of tenure is to insure that infringements of freedom cannot be accomplished with facility or camouflaged under other names. Obviously, students are never eligible for tenure. By definition, they are probationers and must leave after their probative work is done. But the significance of their exclusion from the tenure status should not be overstressed. The profession believes that probationers as well as tenure-holders are entitled to academic freedom, and the gist of its implicit argument is that freedom is a necessity of the office, not a commodity to be earned. True, the non-tenured teacher, under A.A.U.P. rules, may be let go after the expiration of his contract without being given specific charges. But the non-tenured teacher is not procedurally defenseless. Under the same rules, he may challenge the grounds for his non-retention if he feels that they violate academic freedom, and he must be accorded a formal hearing if he can make out a prima-facie case. The student who suspects that he is being punished for his opinions is in somewhat the same position and can justly be granted the same defense.

This would be a minimal extension of due process which, as the

---

[6] In support of a narrow definition, Hook cited an article on academic freedom written for *The Encyclopedia of the Social Sciences* by Professor Arthur O. Lovejoy, the founder of the American Association of University Professors. The citation only partly serves his purpose, for while Lovejoy did distinguish between academic freedom and "political or personal freedom," he also wrote, in lines not quoted, that a violation of the latter would constitute a violation of the "spirit" of the former. The same authority, moreover, can be cited with opposite intent. Lovejoy was the principal author of the 1915 Statement of Principles, and there extramural freedom is assimilated into the larger term. The subsequent declarations of the A.A.U.P. make it even clearer that the public utterances of professors fall under the rubric of academic freedom. Certainly, it has never occurred to Committee A, its committee in charge of investigating violations of academic freedom, that dismissals of professors based on civic actions were beyond its scope, and it would have very little business if it so behaved.

A.A.U.P. acknowledges, serves more than one protective purpose. The association is also aware that in an era of omniscient dossiers, for careers that bank on reputation, for persons who must pursue their calling in an academic institution or usually not at all, a dismissal from a university can be an awful penalty. The severity of the punishment, as well as the importance of the freedom principle, prompted the profession to perfect devices that will guard against malice and mistake. For the same reason, due process is no less imperative for students, even when freedom is not at issue, for they too face the danger of the stalking record and have come to rely on the university for passports to desirable careers.

In addition to misconstruing the reasons for separation, Professor Hook, it seems to me, has also misread its costs. I do not have space to give these costs a complete accounting, but I can, by citing a few examples, show how the guild's possessiveness has proved disserviceable—to the students, to the university, and to itself.

It must be conceded that students have been treated better than might be expected from their professional neglect. Deans can be generous, fair, and rational even without the writ of the A.A.U.P. In a recent study of seventy-two state universities, for example, it was found that fully 84 per cent of them provided hearings for students charged with misconduct. But it would also seem likely that more students would be treated even better if what happened to them had come under the care of the organized profession. The same study also revealed that 43 per cent of the respondents did not try their students on specific charges: for them, evidently, the verb "to hear" had a physiological, not juridical, connotation. In addition, 47 per cent indicated that the roles of judge and prosecutor were combined in the same official person: for them, evidently, the idea of "trial" did not imply any strategies against human bias. The A.A.U.P. has long inveighed against *pro forma* trials for professors; had it concerned itself with students, it might have also taken steps against these anomalies, these all-too-common discrepancies between the substance and the stated form.

And it might have clarified its own thinking in the bargain. In

1940, the A.A.U.P. and a key organization of administrators, the Association of American Colleges, agreed to a Statement of Principles on Academic Freedom and Tenure. As the product of intense negotiations, the statement embodied compromises. But as the product of only two-sided negotiations, these compromises sometimes missed the point. Thus, in one section of this authoritative document, a professional right is defined—"The teacher is entitled to freedom in the classroom"—and then hedged by a curious limitation—"but he should be careful not to introduce into his teaching controversial matter which has no relation to his subject." Seeming to ban the most salutary irrelevancies—the suggestive aside of the gifted teacher, the calculated thrust of the devil's advocate—this admonition appears to incorporate, at the expense of good teaching and of teaching freedom, a fluttery concern for student fragileness. The rationale for extracurricular freedom—which rests on a contrary belief in student toughness—had no expositors at this conference. Consequently, it was more difficult to discover the proper classroom principle, which is not that the teacher should always be dispassionate and germane, but that he should allow students to disagree with him when he is not. The sounder professional rule—lost in the course of narrow bargaining—was that the student should be at liberty to reject what a speaker tells him, always in his own assemblages, and in the classroom when the teacher strays.

Finally, one notes how weakly the guild experience was brought to bear on the tumultuous issues raised at Berkeley. This was not because those issues were so new. Most of them had arisen in academic freedom combats long before the college boy took to politics and long before the multiversity had a name. But those combats had involved professors, and the profession did not readily conjoin the problems of producers and consumers in academe.

Take, for example, the early view of the California administration that, to protect the political neutrality of a state university, it had to prohibit political activities by students on the campus. In its own work, the A.A.U.P. had encountered that assertion many times before and had evolved an almost stock rejoinder: For the sake of academic freedom, as well as for the sake of administrative convenience, the university should preserve its neutrality, not by curbing the political actions of its members, but by publicly disavowing responsibility for them. Neutrality by proscription requires a supervisory apparatus, and raises formidable questions of definition (is the Bancroft Strip a part of the city or the university?); neutrality by disownment is by far the simpler and the safer course. There is no telling whether the California authorities would have adhered to this professional principle if it had been commonly applied to students; but it is at least possible that a line of enlightening precedents would have helped avert an explosive mistake.

Or again, take the assertion of the partisans of the Free Speech Movement that the boundaries of student speech should be drawn by the courts, not the university. This assertion was open to two interpretations, neither in accord with the guild's traditions. It could be interpreted as requiring the university to follow the judgment of the courts in affixing punishments for utterances. The A.A.U.P. has never accepted this position. The university, it has argued, must make freedom an overriding value, the courts may balance it against the interests of national loyalty and the public peace. The university, it has further argued, must defer to the motives of the speaker; the courts may be so preoccupied with consequences as to slight the question of intent. Hence, in defending professors, the association has consistently argued that a conviction of contempt of Congress for refusing to testify before a committee should not be the basis for a dismissal, if the reason for silence is conscientious; and that membership in the Communist Party, though vulnerable to civil penalities, should not in itself be regarded as a capital academic offense. This distinction between the normative concerns of the university and society—which recalls the medieval distinction between the spiritual and temporal authorities—might well be asserted to advantage, if illumination had been borrowed from the professors' files.

Perhaps most partisans of the Free Speech Movement favored the second, and seemingly more liberal, interpretation: that the power to punish students for their utterances should reside exclusively in the courts, and never in the academy. Apparently, this interpretation was adopted by the Berkeley faculty when it resolved that "the content of speech or advocacy should not be restricted by the University"—a statement that would seem to prohibit not merely prior restraints on speech but any disciplinary action over speech. Such a sweeping, self-imposed limitation on the authority of the university had never been urged by the professors' association. Its position (as enunciated in the 1940 statement and recently clarified in the Leo Koch case at Illinois) was that the things professors say may have a bearing on their probity, morality, and competence and as such may be used in evidence against them in a formal academic hearing. Thus has the guild demonstrated its concern with faculty responsibilities as well as with faculty privileges, and its belief that academic freedom does not immunize professional misconduct. To be sure, students are not bound by professional codes of ethics or professional norms of fitness. Still, their words may be clues to character and character remains a valid concern of this or any "spiritual order." Moreover, it is as true of students as professors that utterances are not always communications; sometimes (as in the expression of racial insult) they are assaults in verbal guises and should be as amenable to academic prosecution as any physical attack. Indeed, in the American context, a blanket rule against restricting speech—a limited Germanic disavowal—might well be interpreted as a rule of exclusion, as a bar to the introduction of important evidence in trials concerned with non-speech offenses. The professional experience in this matter does not supply any riskless recipes, but it might have avoided certain dangers if it had been applied to the case at hand.

Only for one set of the many Berkeley issues was there no professional experience to draw upon. Unlike students, professors are not domiciled in an enclave, and active in the world beyond; consequently, this critical question of jurisdiction—"What is the responsibility of the university for politically inspired illegal actions that are mounted on the campus and carried out beyond the walls?"—had not intruded itself in their affairs. If it had, the profession would not have found an easy Solomonic answer. On the one hand, to move against illegalities before they are committed may be to punish the ideas and not the actions: the university would do violence to its best ideals if it stifled students' politics prematurely. On the other hand, it has never been held, even under the medieval two-swords doctrine, that the spiritual authority must be indifferent to the demand for public order; and it can hardly be asserted, in the secular society of today, that the university is free to abet transgressions by shielding them in their early stage. Perhaps the following has the makings of a solution: The university should hold its students to a rule of candor; it should insist that those who are bent on forays should announce what they plan to do; it should punish those who work in secret and take society by surprise. But beyond prohibiting conspiracies, it should not concern itself with the incubation of this type of crime. It should not be a sanctuary for plotters, but neither should it be an arm of the police; it should feel it has discharged its debt to Caesar when it places Caesar's constables on the alert.

■

Have we begun to outlive the causes for separation? There are some indications that we have. For one, with the apparent abatement of its status drive, in turn the result of greater status satisfactions, the profession seems more willing to identify itself with the client group. In partial witness thereof, one may cite the establishment in 1963 of the first A.A.U.P. Committee on Faculty Responsibility for Student Freedom, and the halting efforts of that committee to frame a more integrated policy. A second indication is provided by *Dixon* and *Knight*, the cases I touched upon at the beginning. To be sure, the legal effect of these decisions must still be measured. They may define all the constitutional restraints that will ever be placed on the academic landlord, or they may be the forerunners of more elaborate controls. At the moment, they apply only to public institutions and must await an extension of the "state action" doctrine before they can be applied to private ones. Since part of the rulings were in the form of dicta, some judges may still hold to the notion that students, having no constitutional right to be seen, have no constitutional right to be heard. But the cases are already extremely important in a non-legal sense, as signs of a growing social understanding of the potential conflict between rights and welfare. The adage about the direction of the road paved with good intentions had tended to be forgotten: it had come to seem proper that a person on relief, because he was a recipient of a favor, should submit to invasions of his privacy; or that a hospital, because it dispenses charity, may pay its workers a substandard wage. The larger significance of *Dixon* and *Knight* is that they recognize the latent arbitrariness of institutions of assistance, or, in simpler language, the paradox of evil and good will.

Both *Dixon* and *Knight* involved Negro students expelled from Southern colleges for having participated in freedom rides and sit-ins; clearly, the courts, in defending student freedom, were motivated by a concern for civil rights. And the civil rights movement not only awakened judges to student problems; it awakened students to the problems of their world. It is well understood that new outlets for the dissenting student spirit were provided by the drive for racial justice and that the style of campus disobedience was set by the tactics of that other war. Just now the peace movement is performing a similar paradigmatic and provoking function. But it seems to me that these causes did not originate, much as they stimulated and patterned, a transformation in the student mood. The precondition of a politically active student body is an intellectually serious one. For various reasons—the influx of veterans from the wars; the increase in the number of graduate students, who, with the rise of external sponsorship, have reached critical mass in many places; the greater social heterogeneity of student bodies, especially marked in the ivy citadels; the greater demand of the economy for high professional and academic competence—the student world has much matured. Sizable islands of juvenility of course remain—football is still a rooted sport; but the gaming and ignorant plebe no longer seems to command the student pedestals, and student hostility to the mental life no longer seems massive and devout. I believe that if the current causes were to wither (happily, because their goals will have been attained), the academizing—and hence the politicizing—of American students would continue. One is at liberty to feel cheerless about that prospect and to look back with nostalgia upon the days when students were an alien and alienated breed.

But I see it as holding out hope that a rift in the academy may be mended, and though new divisions may be opened (the generations may always know disunion), they will not be such as make plausible the dictum: "Teachers alone are academically free."

■ Reply: JOHN R. SEARLE

Mr. Metzger argued for reintegrating the concept of student academic freedom into the whole academic freedom of the university, and he offered a historical analysis. I am not competent to comment on the analysis; but I completely agree with his plea for reintegration; I want to extend it. In fact, on the basis of the Berkeley experience, I had a feeling that he was beating a dead horse, or perhaps I should say a straw man named Sydney Hook, and I felt—as a part-time university administrator— as if I were a Washington administrator and someone had said, "Look, the way to solve your problem really is to get independent from the British. You should throw off this colonialist yoke!" My feeling is that in the developing theory of academic freedom we have gone beyond the stage now where it's just a matter of the desirability of extending academic freedom to students. Of course, students should have academic freedom. The question is: What does that mean? What are we going to do with it? How do we live with it? And so there are certain questions that I want to pose, or rather certain comments that I want to make on his paper, really, in the form of questions.

The actual academic freedoms that he lists seem to me rather attenuated. It isn't clear how they give to students adequate freedoms of the sort that we're now actively concerned with. There are such things as classroom autonomy for the teacher, research immunity for the scholar, extramural freedom for the staff member, tenure protection for the highly qualified, and assurance of due process. But really, it wasn't clear to me from his remarks how he wants that applied to the student, and in the way that I think of those freedoms applying to students, it's not nearly enough. This isn't what we were fighting about at Berkeley, and I don't think they're really what the extension of the Berkeley struggle to other campuses is about. Now let me say a bit about what I think it is about.

At one point someone commented on the assumption that we really do have civil liberties in the larger society. In a way, I think that's true in some formal sense, but there is a sense in which it's severely attenuated by all sorts of informal pressures and lack of opportunity. We do offer to our citizens the right of free speech, but if you don't own a newspaper or radio station, if you don't have that kind of a forum, what does it mean? And, in particular, what does it mean if you're employed and you have a family and you join the Communist Party or exercise your free speech in some other spectacularly non-conformist way? You lose your job, your children are bothered at school, your wife has troubles at the supermarket, and so on. There may be no illegal action taken against you, but in order to give real content to the ideal of free speech, it requires a lot more than just guaranteeing certain legal forms. Now, in Berkeley, we tried to give real content to the idea of student free speech on the campus. Tomorrow, I am going to go into some of the difficulties that that involved, but I just want to mention a few now by way of commenting on what I think academic freedom for students really can amount to, and the sorts of problems that are involved which I think go far beyond the somewhat attenuated conception that it seemed to me Mr. Metzger was arguing for.

In order to have free speech, you've got to have more than just a chance to discuss politics in a free way with other students in the basement of Engineering Building. You really have to have a forum. Now we've provided a forum at Berkeley. It consists of microphones, loudspeakers, and other facilities for political organizations—incidentally, at the most heavily trafficked area of the campus—and it goes on all the year around, with the climate there a little different from what it is, say, in Cleveland. And at this moment it's now approaching one o'clock in Berkeley, and a speaker of one or another degree of radical opinion is perhaps exhorting students on the Sproul Hall plaza to some form of civil disobedience or other. (I say this just on the basis of induction by simple enumeration.) But this creates certain problems, some of which Mr. Metzger touched on only briefly. How does the university respond when the forum is used not only as a vehicle for exhortation, but positively in terms of large-scale organization? How does it deal with what last year we called, with Freudian directness, the "mounting problem"? Originally this problem arose out of a futile attempt to distinguish between advocacy and mounting.

Let me explain what this means in practical terms. On the night of October 15 a march was organized on the campus, and the position that I took as a short-term university administrator was that the university is not responsible for what the students do off the campus, and it's not responsible for their opinions. But in real life it really is a very interesting intellectual problem to try to make that stick. The students were denied parade permits by both Berkeley and Oakland, and they were rather numerous. About 10,000 or so assembled for the march, and some estimates were as high as 15,000, by for example the *San Francisco Examiner* (which is a Hearst newspaper—and not anxious to overestimate the power of the student movement). The students assembled on the campus, and following our policies of free speech, we made certain special provisions by way of erecting speakers' platforms, special microphones, an extra loud-speaker system, gates to handle the crowds, not to mention hot dog stands to provide them with food, etc. Now notice what we did. We allowed the launching of a peripatetic demonstration of 10,000 or more into the dark with no destination and no plan for dispersal; and thousands of hostile members of the John Birch Society and other lively California groups were waiting for them. And the position that I have argued and fought for all year is that we did the right thing.

But there is a certain question which we're really going to have to confront. To what extent does our very attempt to give content to the formal guarantees of free speech, by providing active mechanisms for exercising free speech and political organization, involve us in a kind of complicity? And it's terribly difficult to stick by our first principle, that the content of what is being advocated is of no interest to us. Suppose an extremist element in the student movement, the element that really wanted violence with the police, had gained control? Suppose the movement had not been in the control of the moderates? And suppose that it looked like we might have violence right on the edge of the campus—that the police would have been there instead of a few blocks away? Then I think our problem would have been one of making very difficult and delicate political decisions of a kind that are really not solved for us by Mr. Metzger's list of classroom autonomy for the teacher, extramural freedom for the students, nor by his brief discussion of the organizing problem. Notice that in such cases there is no question of foreknowledge versus secrecy. Everybody knows what is going on, because it is impossible to organize such mass actions in secret.

How do we work out in practice the decision that we made in Berkeley last year? And how are other universities going to work this out in practice in such a way that we do actively maintain freedom of speech? We grant much more freedom of speech, really, than is available in the society at large, because there's no other forum in California comparable to the one that we offer on the Sproul Hall steps. The rest of California is, incidentally, finding this out and they're flocking to the Sproul Hall steps. How do we handle that in such a way that we do not compromise the university politically, and that we do not in any way interfere with or impede the educational processes of the university? That's the sort of question I am left with after having heard Mr. Metzger's very eloquent plea for extending academic freedom to students.

One final remark. Mr. Metzger has at least partly misinterpreted the famous Berkeley faculty resolution of December 8. He seems to think it implies or could imply that nothing a student says can be used as evidence against him in a trial. But this is not true. The December 8 resolution implies that the university should have no rules prohibiting students from expressing certain views or advocating certain courses of action. But, for example, a student's declaration of intent to violate a rule can be used against him as evidence in a hearing concerning his violation of that rule, and nothing in the December 8 resolution implies otherwise. The prohibition of rules against speech does not imply a prohibition of the use of speech to ascertain the existence of violations of other rules.

■ DISCUSSION

W. METZGER: Mr. Searle and I seem unable to astonish one another. He finds my arguments for reintegrating student and professor freedoms sound but rather obvious. I find his assertion that the effective exercise of freedom needs something more than the absence of restraint true but rather truistic. He holds that my principles do not yield solutions to emergencies of the Berkeley type. I doubt that his own formulation offers an exact recipe for action. It may be, of course, that we both underestimate the distance between freedom analyzed abstractly and freedom administered in the pinch.

Does Mr. Searle also mean to imply, by his allusions to dead horses and straw men, that the issues that concern me are no longer viable? If he really believes that the custodial interests of the university no longer impinge on student freedom, or that the guild is no longer reluctant to share its privileges with its clients, or even that the A.A.U.P. doctrine of academic freedom no longer poses analytic difficulties, I would have to say that it is he, not I, who is out of touch with academic realities. Berkeley, at this moment, may have its mind on other things. But Berkeley does not typify the nation; moreover, Berkeley today is not the rule-ridden place it was two years ago. To think it represents a prevailing or even imminent condition is to betray the blindness of the newly fortunate.

Let me tell you about a case that was recently brought to the attention of the American Civil Liberties Union—perhaps significantly, the victim, a student, did not direct his appeal to the professors' association. Some months ago, this student was expelled by his college for having grown a beard. He was given no chance to explain himself: the authorities apparently concluded that his culpability was written on his face. This case may strike you as humorous or inconsequential. But I regard it as serious and symptomatic. The absence of due process gives me one large cause for concern. Where, if not in colleges, can we expect that personal accusations will be tested in a fair and impartial manner; where, if not in academic situations, can we expect human contact to be courteous and decent? The grounds for the expulsion give me even greater concern. Wherein did the beard offend? Did the authorities oppose it for aesthetic reasons? Then they should have been humble enough to restrain themselves, for one man's eyesore can be another man's ornament and no man should lay down rules about good looks. Or did they oppose the beard for political reasons? Did they regard it as an expression of an allegiance or of an opinion, rather like an armband or a rosary? Then they should have been conscious of the academic-freedom issue and should have revered the beard. I am not suggesting that all unshaven students are perilously at the razor's edge. But no one familiar with the conventional operations of academe would consider this institution's dictatorial insistence that everyone wear a middle-class uniform a very unusual thing. The fight for enlightened neglect—which Mr. Searle would seem to class among remembrances of things past—is far from over.

J. SEARLE: I must hasten to reassure Mr. Metzger that I do not suppose Berkeley is a typical American college. Far from it. Nor am I surprised to hear of the existence of incidents of the sort he describes. My point is that the most difficult intellectual problems—problems of analyzing the proper relations between freedom and order in real empirical contexts in the mid-1960's—do not now concern what I take to be the somewhat timid approach of arguing that students should have the A.A.U.P. conception of classroom freedom that professors have traditionally fought for. I know of only one serious thinker in the United States—and he is perhaps not to be taken too seriously—who denies the desirability of extending these sorts of freedoms to students.

What I was arguing is that the contemporary intellectual problems have to do with a much more expansive notion of freedom. It is not a matter simply of leaving people alone; it is not enough for the university simply to adopt a hands-off policy. I think the university is under an obligation actually to attempt to facilitate the exercise of freedoms. In society at large there is a crucial distinction between the formal freedoms guaranteed in law and the Constitution and the actual freedoms which it is possible to exercise. The formal freedoms can easily become meaningless in a large, heavily industrialized, highly technological society of 200,000,000 people, where the means of communication are not available to any but a very small minority. There are, furthermore, very effective but also very subtle forms of discouraging the positive exercise of freedom in such a society. Non-conformity can be discouraged with very genteel punishments. If free speech is to be meaningful there have to be effective opportunities to communicate and protection for dissenters. These are what the university needs to provide for its students (and incidentally faculty) on the campus.

P. GOODMAN: Wouldn't you say, though, that society as a whole should provide that? Hyde Park in London is so beyond anything we have in the United States, and I don't see why it's just the Berkeley campus that should have that, you know, rather than the city of Cleveland.

J. SEARLE: There are things that I think society ought to do that we are now doing on the Berkeley campus. Absolutely! The point here about our forum is that it is an extremely effective organizational device. You can organize a strike, a sit-in, a march, or a political campaign. The Sproul plaza is for that reason an important element in California politics.

■

While I don't have enough data about what the student leaders are like nationally, one of our problems in Berkeley is that a lot of student leadership talent feels so alienated from the whole system—not just the university but the whole structure of American society—that they don't want to have anything to do with the official organizational forms, which they think, often really in a kind of paranoid way, are all part of the military-industrial complex. And I think one of the things we must do in a university is make the official mechanisms of the university seem appealing in a way that will attract genuine student leadership talent from the entire spectrum of the student activists. We're doing that in the student newspaper. The radicals have their columns and the reactionaries have their columns, and so on. So it is something that we're working on and succeeding in. But I don't know how the other universities are.

P. GOODMAN: It's obvious that if the student government has no powers allotted to it constitutionally—you know, it's simply to decide on the pin and the boat ride—the most intellectually energetic students will certainly not be concerned with rising in that department, and those who do rise up are those who for the most part like to play at political games, and often go right on to become district attorneys or governors. That's what they're good at. But they're not good at any real social function. Well, of course, this is a very mixed thing. The San Francisco State student government has now won the right to appoint a professor or two which they pay for out of student dues. You see, they just assess the students each a dollar and then they pay a professor. Then they begin to have much more substantive power. You know, they are using that tax function for something besides the boat ride. When that begins to become the case then there will be better student leadership.

S. KADISH: In Berkeley what happened was that this very important student movement occurred outside the structure of the existing student government; that was completely by-passed. Indeed, the regular student government was looked down upon by these active students as what they referred to as "sandbox" government, and deprecated.

J. SEARLE: The main problem is to revise the whole structure and conception of student government so that it will attract better people, and make a more serious contribution to running the university.

III

III

☐ Essay: JOHN R. SEARLE

       To me, the more fascinating aspects of political theory concern not the abstract statement of the goals of the *polis* but the application of the abstract theory to empirical situations. Similarly with theories of the university. Our problem is not so much to articulate an objective or set of objectives for the institution as to relate those abstract objectives to the concrete problems that are now confronting American universities. The classical political theorists, e.g., Locke, Hobbes, and Rousseau, had a relatively simple and easy solution to the political-theory problem: they postulated a more or less fixed human nature and an account of the origins of society—all on very weak empirical grounds—and then derived the character of political organization from the postulates. Our problem is not going to be solved so easily, for the problems facing American universities are now changing so rapidly that even in cases where people have had enough sense to base their theories of the university on a careful appraisal of the facts, the appraisals are soon out of date; and even such a sophisticated piece of technological determinism as Kerr's *Uses of the University* is now, in some crucial respects at least, obsolete. This book is, incidentally, a brilliant work; there are just two things wrong with it. One is, if you read it you have the feeling: Why bother? If that is all that the university amounts to, why would anyone want to devote his life to it? And secondly, Kerr seems to have neglected, though not forgotten, the fact that there are also students in the university. And I would say that what happened in Berkeley last year might, in a sense, be regarded as a kind of empirical refutation of the theory, the crucial experiment testing that account of the university, or "multiversity," as it came to be called. Kerr predicted a possible revolt of students against the faculty. What actually happened was a revolt of students—and faculty—against the administration.

Well, anyway, let's start with the easy task—the abstract statement of the goals. The purpose of the university is the advancement and dissemination of knowledge. Now I've heard that so often at Berkeley that I'm beginning really to doubt that it's true. But in the end and after a lot of agonizing I really will come out for that. The purpose of the university is the advancement and dissemination of knowledge. And it *is* very controversial—I can't convince a lot of my students that that *is* the purpose of the university. It amounts to, in less euphemistic terminology, "teaching and research." With one arm you try to tell these kids something and with the other arm you try to write another article for the journals. The university is an institutional form devised to produce these two related objectives. In order that they should be achieved, certain kinds of insulation and independence from society are necessary. And among the elements of this insulation is what is known as academic freedom. In order that teaching and research may be effectively pursued they have to be pursued independently of outside interference. This conception gives us what I would call the "minimalist" or "A.A.U.P." or "special" theory of academic freedom. Academic freedom is derived from and is restricted to the special needs of the academy. It consists only of such freedoms as are necessary to protect teaching and research. Rationally this conception seems to me to apply both to the teacher's freedom to study and teach and to the student's freedom to study and learn. So, in the manner of the classical philosophers, we derive from the essential purposes of the institution—teaching and research—the sorts of liberties necessary to its effective functioning.

But there is another and, I think, larger conception of academic freedom that I will come to shortly. Around this institution, and in America really within the institution, there springs up a community; and the members of this campus community have inter-

ests, needs, and purposes other than simply education and research—and how they do! People eat, sleep, work, join trade
unions, go to football games, engage in political activities, and
generally behave in the ways that the members of a community
do—at least partly, and in some respects largely, independently of
the teaching and research functions of the university. Now, what
should be the relations between this community and the central
functions of the university? Well, the traditional American answer
to that is that the university is *in loco parentis* over the student
members of the community. The university is the (authoritarian)
parent and the students are the (docile) children of this parent.
For a complex set of historical reasons, the doctrine of *in loco
parentis* no longer works. Particularly it does not work on campuses with large graduate-student populations. Where you have
students, say, twenty-seven years old or even older, conducting
advanced research, finishing doctoral dissertations, and raising
families, it is impossible plausibly to say to them: "The university
is your surrogate father; it has the same kind of authority over you
your father did when you were a child." So *in loco parentis* is
dead. Oh, it's not dead in the ideology of some administrators, but
as an operational theory for running big campuses of the kind I am
familiar with, it simply does not work. They tried to make it work
in Berkeley in 1964—and it was a spectacular failure.

But now an interesting thing is: So far no new ideology has
really replaced *in loco parentis*. Nobody knows where we are now.
The one we are experimenting with in Berkeley might be characterized as follows: The general principle for regulating the campus
community is that the freedoms of the campus community are the
same as those of the larger surrounding community, with the
proviso that rules are set up (preferably rules made by the people
that are going to be governed by those rules) regulating what we
call the "time, place, and manner" (another phrase I'm beginning
to get suspicious of) of student and faculty activities; such rules
exist to prevent the interference of these activities with education
and research and subsidiary functions of the university—and subsidiary functions are fairly broadly conceived so as to include the
protection of aesthetic sensibilities, and other such matters. I think
this theory is intellectually unexceptionable. It takes some working

out, but it can be done. What this amounts to really is that anything goes as long as it is legal and it does not interfere with the normal functions of the university, in some fairly loose and *ad hoc* sense of "interfere" and some even looser sense of "function." What is illegal off the campus is illegal on the campus, but by the same token the rights you have off the campus, or anyway the rights you're supposed to have off the campus (even if you don't really have them!) you have *on* the campus. The university is not a sanctuary, but it's not a prison either.

Now, underlying this approach, I think, is a different conception of academic freedom, which I would call a "maximalist" or "general" or "FSM" theory, as opposed to the "A.A.U.P." or "special" or "minimalist" theory, of academic freedom. Academic freedom is simply the normal freedoms of a democratic society as applied to and shaped by the specific needs of the academy—with the addition, in our case at least, of the active participation of the academy in providing the vehicles for exercising this freedom (and that really is a special problem I'm going to say something about later). While the special theory seeks to justify academic freedoms in terms of the purposes of the university, the general theory takes freedom for granted and insists that any restrictions on the freedoms of members of the campus community be justified in terms of the functions of the university. So the special theory justifies freedom; the general theory assumes freedom and insists on justifications of any restrictions on freedom. These two conceptions are not mutually exclusive, nor, properly conceived, are they inconsistent. They are not competing answers to the same question, but they are non-competing answers to two different questions. The special theory asks, "What justification can we give for freedom within the university?" and the general theory asks, "What justification can we give for any restrictions on freedom within the university?" And really, whether you invoke one or the other, I think, often depends on various kinds of political considerations, whom you are arguing with and for what purposes. But what is relatively new, I think, in the present situation, is the attempt to regulate a university on the rather libertarian assumptions of the second approach. So that instead of the authoritarian idea of *in loco parentis* we are trying to run a university on the assumptions of the general theory that all restrictions on liberty have to be justified on certain fairly specific grounds.

On ideological grounds I think that this statement of principles is unexceptionable—in fact, I spent several months of my life fighting for it. But the question we are now facing in Berkeley is whether or not it can be made to work in practice in a large state university in the United States. The situation, to make another political analogy, is not completely unlike that of the Fourth Republic in France. The Fourth Republic had a pretty good constitution, rather better, in fact, than the constitution of the Fifth Republic from the point of view of the ideals of liberal democracy. But there were, unfortunately for political philosophy, certain empirical features of social life in France that made it unstable to the point of collapse. One set of problems of the Berkeley administration is to stave off similar instabilities in our situation, and I want now to describe two forces for instability in our present situation.

Put bluntly and crudely, the difficulty with the general proposal I just outlined is that the students don't want it and the public won't stand for it. A large sub-set of the students, and this includes many very able students, reject the fundamental assumption of the above analysis, that the primary functions of the university are education and research; and, secondly, it is becoming increasingly clear that the public, and by that I mean to include also the Regents, alumni, and state government, will not tolerate the political and social consequences of the kind of libertarianism implicit in the general theory of academic freedom. First, I'm going to talk about the students; then I'm going to talk about the public. I am going to spend most of the time on the students because all of you know about the public and have strong feelings about the public, but maybe I'll say something about students that you will take exception to. You are likely to agree with what I say about the public, so I will not spend much time on it. I am talking about Berkeley, but I don't think I'm really talking just about Berkeley; I think in a way I am talking about American higher education. It's true that this is a megalomaniac disease we suffer from at Berkeley—we really think we are the wave of the future— but in certain respects I think the problems we have, to put it in more academic terminology, are likely to be faced by other universities similar to ours. I realize that sounds rather tautological, but I think there is some content to it nonetheless.

Student life at Berkeley and other such universities may be divided roughly into five cultures.[1] The divisions I am going to present are very rough, and I do not suppose there are very many people that represent pure types, so I'm going to give you some archetypes, caricatures. But I think they do mark important divisions in the student body. And don't take the labels too seriously; I'll explain what I mean by the labels.

First there is a *fraternity-sorority culture.* I do not mean by this label that all of the members of this culture are in fraternities or sororities, but rather there is a culture which centers around fraternities and sororities and which embraces a certain conception of undergraduate life long familiar on campuses all over the country. In Berkeley this culture is dwindling in size, and psychologically it is very much on the defensive. For example, one fraternity has already closed this semester and several others are in desperate straits. It is incredible for somebody who went to a state university at the time that I did to think that these institutions are, and this whole conception of undergraduate life is, weakening, possibly dying. But this is the case. I have hated this style of undergraduate life so long that the idea that it might actually disappear is really terribly depressing. But anyway, I don't think we need to worry about this culture too much because it has lost much of its vigor. Maybe it will have a resurgence, but I do not see it in the near future.

Secondly, there is a *professional culture* of students whose college years are oriented toward their future careers. For them, the university is a means to a professional end. This culture embraces most of the students in law, engineering, forestry, business administration, and pre-medicine; many graduate students, especially in the applied sciences; and students in other professionally oriented programs.

Thirdly, there is an *intellectual culture* (there really *is*, contrary to what a lot of professors think) of students who see knowledge

[1] For certain suggestions in the taxonomy which follows I am indebted to Professor Martin Trow.

and understanding as ends in themselves and tend to regard their successes in the university in terms of their own intellectual development. Many of these people aspire to academic careers. They make up a large proportion of the graduate students, especially in the humanities and in certain of the social sciences.

But now we come to the crunch. Fourth and fifth are the *political culture* and the *bohemian culture*. Now don't take this last word too seriously, but it is the best one I could think of. "Beatnik" is a bit vulgar and the other words I could think of are in various ways even more unsatisfactory. These two cultures represent the peculiar element in the present historical situation, especially in Berkeley, but I think in other large American universities as well. I'll talk about them at a little more length. (Parenthetically, let me insert that there is a sixth culture of the culturally apathetic, a large undifferentiated mass who spend a lot of time in front of television sets and who provide a source of recruits for the other five cultures.) Faculty and administrative understanding of the political and bohemian cultures are generally quite inadequate. Professors tend to perceive the political culture in terms of their own student days spent either as campus liberals or as young Marxists. Both such models are now obsolete. Just so, with equal irrelevance, the faculty often tend to perceive the bohemian culture in terms of an outdated student bohemia, in terms of the pre-pot, pre-LSD bohemian cultures of their own student days on the GI Bill in Paris or in Greenwich Village or in some other bohemian shelter.

The characteristic feature of the political culture, for purposes of our present discussion, is that the practitioners of this culture regard the university primarily as a base for organizing and launching political activity. That is, they reject the assumption that the purposes of the university are education and research, in favor of the view that the main purpose of the university is to effect social change. The political activists reject the underlying assumption of the abstract theory of the university in a way that none of the groups previously discussed do. Furthermore, the radical element in the political culture, and it is this element which at present tends to dominate and lead the entire culture, has certain other peculiar features.

First, they reject the political assumptions behind what for want of a better phrase I will call the "liberal establishment" in this country. That is, they reject the assumption that politics is best conducted by compromise, conciliation, negotiation, and discussion. They reject these methods in favor of more apocalyptic forms of political activity. Their strategy is to polarize issues on moral grounds, so that last year, for example, every time a new compromise was proposed and every time the Regents made another concession, it was always described as "horrendous." This got to be a favorite word. And the point here is that movements like this exist by polarizing the issues, by making issues seem as far apart as they possibly can and as black and white as they possibly can, between absolute moral purity and absolute black immorality. The style of the discussion which goes with this is absolutist, emotional, and moralizing. It is a lot of fun, but it is not the style of liberal-establishment politics, and much less is it the style of academic discussion. And furthermore, the practitioners of this particular style of politics are rather eager to resort to direct action and confrontation. They have found a good weapon; it works well and they are anxious to try it out. Sometimes even in silly ways. For instance, at the beginning of this semester a lot of people were anxious to have the student book store become a discount store. Well, the question was: Should we sit in, or do we have a shop-in, or what kind of direct action will make the move from non-discount to discount? This amounts to a kind of parody of the civil rights movement.

Secondly, and this is important, the politics of the political activists is now non-ideological, indeed positively anti-ideological! We have in a sense come full circle from the utopian socialists. For about a century Marx convinced people that radical movements require a coherent ideology, a "scientific" theory of society on which to base political action. An important factor in the history of political radicalism in the past century has been the assumption that the attempt to build radical movements simply on moral indignation, without an underlying theory of social change, was naive, unscientific, utopian, and rather childish. But now, it is ideological politics which are regarded as "square," and the attempt is being made to build a revolutionary movement on successive waves of moral indignation without any underlying abstract or metaphysical theory of society and historical change. Like the utopian socialists, the present student political radicals in general tend to engage in a politics of moral outrage, not a politics of ideological analysis.

Notice that as a consequence of all this the campus political movement is in a certain sense profoundly anti-intellectual, or to put it more circumspectly, non-intellectual. Knowledge is seen as valuable only as a basis for action and it is not even terribly important there; far more important than what one knows is how one feels. It is a politics of feeling rather than of intellectual analysis. When Paul Goodman came to Berkeley last winter I remember he remarked with some surprise on the intellectual shallowness of the FSM's literary output. It seemed to me that an observer as shrewd as he is should have noticed that the superficiality of the propaganda really was a natural consequence of the non-intellectual and anti-theoretical style of the FSM. Now, I am not knocking the FSM; I thought it was a marvellous movement in many ways, but it did not happen to be an intellectual movement. It was, in a rather deep sense, a non-intellectual movement of intellectuals, a movement of intelligent people who reject certain assumptions about theoretical knowledge.

I will not dwell long on the bohemian culture, though it is important to make clear that it is not the same as the political culture. Its main features are non-conformity and experimentalism in matters of dress, aesthetics, drugs, sex, and social relations. It shares with large elements of the political culture a profound sense of alienation from American society in general and from the university in particular. Tactically speaking, it provides a ready source of recruits for the political radicals, particularly where more spectacular forms of direct action are involved. If the political radicals are willing to organize the march, the bohemians will happily march. The converse, incidentally, does not hold, so that last year, though the FSM had the support of the bohemians, when some of the social non-conformists tried to organize the so-called "obscenity" issue, they got very little support from the political radicals of the FSM.

Now, the existence of these two cultures in fairly large numbers

(and, incidentally, tacked onto them is a large non-student population of hangers-on, especially in the bohemian culture) faces the
university with a certain kind of built-in instability. It means that
there are hundreds of students, and perhaps even thousands of
students, who reject the view that the functions of the university
are or should be or can be education and research, but who are
quite intelligent people. As a consequence of this, we are in the
usual position of American universities of having thousands of
intelligent people who really ought not to be in the university
because they are unsuited for the peculiar nature of the university
as an institution. This is the point that Paul has made often, that a
university is a specialized institution. It is specialized in the way
that a hospital is specialized. Not everybody feels that he has to be
in the hospital just to be in the hospital. But pretty much everybody in our society feels that if he can get in he has to be in a
university. Not only is there the traditional American conception
that everybody must have a degree, but there are also the desires to
avoid the draft, to postpone career decisions, to continue the free
and easy life of the youth culture into one's late twenties, to use
the university as a basis for organizing radical movements, and so
on. A lot of people are in a university because they can't bear the
thought of being anywhere else in the United States. But now we
come to the crunch; now we come to the difficult part, and that is:
The traditional ways that an American university has of coping
with students who, though they are intelligent, really have no
business in a university are quite ineffective in dealing with these
groups. The traditional extracurricular activities are of little or no
interest to them. Furthermore, the promise of future success if
only they will play the academic game, now ("You're going to be
a really great insurance salesman if you'll only buckle down and
learn accounting *now*"), really has no appeal; it just does not work
at all as a way of domesticating these groups. How should the
university deal with the sort of problems posed by such groups?

There are two approaches that we are now working on. First,
one can attempt to assimilate political activism into the university
by treating it as just another form of student extracurricular activity. Just as the fraternity-sorority culture requires active complicity
from the university in order to have such things as football games,

so the university satisfies the political culture by providing a forum, complete with microphone, speaker's platform, etc., for the extracurricular activities of the political culture. This answer is an attempt to apply the maximalist theory of academic freedom I outlined above. One assimilates the political culture, and with it the activist tendencies of the bohemian culture, to the academic milieu by treating politics as just one more extracurricular activity, but so regulated that it does not interfere with the normal primary functions of the university. We have a hiking club, a chess club, and a Viet Nam protest club, all regulated by the same rules. To the astonishment of my conservative colleagues on the faculty, this assimilationist solution is actually working out rather well. Political radicalism is more and more becoming just a kind of extracurricular activity that happens to go on in Berkeley and in other major universities.

But it does present certain problems. First, the most convenient target of the political activists is the university itself; so that, for example, when there are arrests in Bogalusa, picket signs go up outside of Sproul Hall (because the university buys paper from Crown-Zellerbach—and I have even heard plans now for some kind of a flush-in). Indeed, the revolutionary element tends to regard the university itself as part of the "military-industrial complex," often in a ludicrous way. People sometimes come into my office and say things like, "Searle, you've made yourself an agent of the military-industrial complex," and I guess they intend that as more than a joke. Anyway, this identification leads some constantly to seek ways to undermine the university, and more importantly, to make constant efforts to place the students in an adversary role against the administration and, to a lesser extent, the faculty. The effect of this is that there is a constant struggle for power within the university between the radical elements of the student population on the one hand and the administration and faculty on the other. Maybe to a certain extent this is healthy but after a time it does get to be rather a bore.

Now, secondly, the intense level of political activity is regarded by some people as threatening what used to be called the atmosphere of the campus. Some faculty members feel that universities should be quiet, peaceful places where they can get a lot of work done. At present, in the eyes of some at least, Berkeley is not such a place. Maybe these faculty members who want peace and quiet are unjustified, but right now the fact that they *want* peace and quiet and are simultaneously in demand at other universities is an important datum in the calculation of any university administration.

The third problem with the political culture is that non-students tend to move in on it in various ways. It is such an inviting target for political forces off the campus that it's really rather difficult for a full-time student to maintain control of a serious and important student political organization. Often student political leaders drop out of school to become full-time organizers. In the grape strike the strike leaders came to the campus, the student organizations gave them their use of the microphones, and the strike leaders then organized on campus for a strike that was going on hundreds of miles away. They got many students to participate in the strike, even though superficially it would seem that students are somewhat unrelated to it. And fourthly, and this is in a way the worst problem, it appears that the public is not going to stand for the consequences of the maximalist theory; I'll say something about this later.

Now I wish to turn from this brief summary of the assimilationist approach and the problems it poses to a second, complementary, and more daring approach. Besides treating activism as just one form of extracurricular activity among others, why not try assimilating at least certain elements of it as part of the regular academic program? For example, if the same impulses that lead a student to sit in at a car agency because it refuses to hire Negroes will lead him to teach illiterate children in Oakland how to read, or teach trigonometry to high school students living in slums, or work in a mental hospital, or in a drug-addiction program, then why not provide facilities that will enable him to perform such activities, and indeed why not provide university credit for such activities, at least to the extent that they have some intellectual content? True, this involves relaxing what many people regard as traditional standards of academic purity, for it is important to emphasize that such activities should not be confined to students majoring in education or social welfare or criminology. I am not proposing simply to extend the scope of academically rewarded field work for future social-welfare professionals, but to give academic credit to English majors and engineers who want to improve the society they live in. The history of American universities suggests that relaxing academic purity for some utilitarian ends is dangerous, but nonetheless I think it is worth the risks and indeed presents exciting possibilities for satisfying very deeply felt needs, for putting activist energies into what administrators like to call "constructive channels," and possibly even for opening up some new and interesting conceptions of what higher education can be. The scope of such possible community-service activities is wide and the eagerness of students to engage in it is steadily growing. But such activities take more time and resources than students characteristically have. The university can provide the resources (public money is available for such projects), and by giving academic credit it can in effect provide the time.

Finally, I want to discuss the problem of the public's response to the university. The paradox here is that even when the university succeeds in domesticating the impulses I have been discussing so that they do not interfere with the functions of the institution, it seems that these very successes only increase public hostility. One problem, of course, is the old inability of many to discriminate between providing a forum and taking responsibility for the views expressed in the forum. Many American universities have this problem. A Communist is invited to speak on the campus and people take that as an endorsement by the university of the Communist point of view. The only way to deal with this is to keep repeating over and over the obvious distinction between providing a free forum and endorsing the views expressed in the forum.

There is a second and harder problem, the problem of organization. This problem concerns the responsibility of the university for major assaults on the community organized on and launched from the campus. Intellectually it poses itself as follows: It is impossible to make a distinction between advocacy and organization. Freedom of advocacy necessarily involves freedom to organize. I am convinced of this on both philosophical and political grounds. But the requirements of the general theory I enunciated earlier require a forum for advocacy and that means a forum for organization. But if you provide the forum for organization, so that the idea of free speech really becomes politically meaningful, then it is much harder to disclaim responsibility for the consequences of the organization. If you provide the facilities to organize, say, ten thousand people to stage an illegal march or some other form of illegal mass direct action against the community, it is much harder to disclaim any responsibility, because it is always arguable that the assault could not have taken place if you had not gone out of your way to provide certain kinds of facilities. It is impossible to get ten thousand people together and organize them to take concerted action unless certain special arrangements have been made by way of providing speakers' platforms, microphones with loud-speakers, and so on. Now, we require student organizations to pay for these. They pay any extra costs incurred by the university for special events, and that makes the taxpayers feel a little bit better. But the fact remains that mass illegal actions take place only because the university provides the facilities for organizing them, and this is a source not only of intellectual interest to philosophers like myself but of anxiety and hostility toward the university on the part of many people outside the institution.

Intellectually, the way out of this problem is to point out that there is still a valid distinction between providing a forum open to everybody, and being responsible for the actual consequences produced by certain groups that use that forum. This distinction is implicit in the constitutionally valid distinction between the act of advocacy and the act advocated. Often the act of advocacy is legal and constitutionally protected even in cases where the act advocated is illegal. So the principle that students have their constitutional rights of free speech on the campus forbids the university from interfering with advocacy (and hence, organization) even in cases where the act advocated is illegal. Furthermore, the constitutionally touchy area of criminal conspiracy and solicitation is obviously a matter for courts and not for university administrators to adjudicate. But though this is, or may be, a correct point of view it does not reassure the general public much.

Incidentally, this area is not without its comic possibilities. When the first large Viet Nam Day March was organized and 14,000 people marched off the campus, a professor of mathematics active in the VDC announced beforehand that they intended to invade the Oakland Army Terminal "by land, sea, and air." If we had any sense of humor left in California that would rank as a classic statement, but the level of ability to detect preposterousness has gone so far down that the announcement only increased the general hysteria.

Oddly enough, many elements in the general public do not even like the idea of students doing community-service work of the kind I described earlier. Much less do they like the idea of giving university credit for it. The Synanon drug-addiction program, which for a time worked closely with campus groups, is very controversial (that's another word we hear a lot now!); and the idea that students are going to be actively working for desegregated housing or are going to challenge the validity of the Oakland schools by calling attention to the fact that tenth-graders are, as they say, "functionally illiterate"—all such things produce a good deal of hostility in the community.

One last problem with the public results from these others. The university itself becomes a political issue, one of the hottest political issues, if not the hottest, in the entire state. Opportunistic candidates exploit and increase public hostility to the university and present officeholders grow increasingly nervous as they are identified with the alleged subversive activities on the campus. I think that in order to cope with this we, that is, the administration of the university, are going to have to engage in a much more active program of public education than we ever have. We are going to have to actively lobby, inform, explain, and justify to the public what the ideals of a university are and what value the university represents to the community. In particular, we are going to have to explain two principles: the first is that the university does not interfere with freedom of expression, and the second is that our regulations are designed to prevent interference with the normal functions of the university, and not to make us surrogate parents. It is those two principles, both parts of the maximalist theory of academic freedom, that we are trying to live with now.

■ Reply: WALTER P. METZGER

Someone—I think it was a German traveler —once called America the land of the overrated child. After listening to this talk, I would be inclined to improve the aphorism: America, first and foremost, is the land of the underrated young adult.

One could cite many examples of how we grade people down as they grow up. We value expressiveness in the young up to the time when it grows erotic; then we impose constraints. We take mental independence in a child of eight to be a happy omen, and then call it troublesome and neurotic when it shows up ten years hence. We do all we can to remove frustrations from the nursery, the playground, the grade school; then we seem to do all we can to insert frustrations into the graduate school, the army camp, and the beginning job.

Mr. Searle does not explicitly endorse this animus. Quite the contrary. As a faculty member, his sympathies were with the young adults who defended their rights and interests through the Free Speech Movement. His current intentions as an administrator, as described in this engaging paper, are not only libertarian but compassionate. Yet I detect in his discussion of the student radicals an undertone of depreciation that seems all the more indicative of a pervasive bias because it comes from an advocate of their rights. He terms the style of contemporary student politics "apocalyptic" and "moralistic," among other things. But he says nothing about the content of that politics. As it happens, that politics is mostly about a potentially apocalyptic war and a great moral objective—racial justice. The nature of the outer world shapes the style of this political response: to ignore this is to place distorting emphasis on the vagaries of the students' psyches.

Mr. Searle calls this political sub-culture "anti-intellectual." That term is used loosely in common parlance, but it ought to be used precisely in a setting where it is able to convey so much opprobrium. It is not the equivalent of "superficial." I do not doubt that the statements of the Free Speech leaders and of some of the New Leftists now are often less than profound. But if that were a basis for chastisement, most of their professors some of the time and some of their professors most of the time would also deserve a good whipping. It is not a synonym for "anti-ideological." Indeed, insofar as intellectuality presupposes a certain playfulness with ideas, a rigid piety about ideas would more accurately connote its absence. It may be plausibly defined as an attitude of hostility toward intellectuals. But, when so defined, the term does not seem to me well applied. I find at Columbia (can the world of the Pacific be vastly different?) that, except for a small minority at the rabid edges, the more politically radical the student is, the more likely he is to respect the academic intellectual—that teacher who has the appetite and the knack for turning old solutions into new uncertainties. The student who cares nothing about politics, or who cares in an entirely passive way, is more likely, I find, to approve the lecturer who transmits the conventional wisdom and expedites his passage through the college maze.

Is the world of the Pacific vastly different? Yes, probably, in that it assembles a larger population at the extremes. But I have deduced from my own observations of it—admittedly these are small-ranged and fragmentary—that it does have similarities with the other coast. I gave a talk at Berkeley the very night it was plunged into one of its darkest crises by the resignation of its president and chancellor. Forsaken by my faculty hosts, who had rushed off to save the university once again, I was about to return alone to my hotel room when a graduate student in the audience invited me to join him and others for beer and conversation at a local pub. I soon discovered that my companions had taken part in the Free Speech sit-in, had participated in racial demonstrations, and had, if not the full panoply of attitudes of the New Left, at least a good number of its commitments. I thought it significant, however, that these concerns did not preoccupy us. We spent five minutes talking about the "industrial-military complex," ten minutes talking about student freedom, and the rest of the time talking about their dissertations, which most of them regarded as interesting and "relevant," and about their careers, which most of them intended to be academic. Even granting the fortuitousness of the sample, I am inclined to believe that these students were not eccentric, and that three of Mr. Searle's archetypes—the professional, the intellectual, and the political—do in fact greatly overlap. If I were to attempt categorical separations—and I do think these "caricatures" can be useful—I would distinguish, more sharply than Mr. Searle has done, the solipsistic consciousness of the bohemians from the external reference of the politicals. The "beat" world draws upon itself, and vanity, which is its prime commodity, is exhausting; the political world reaches out to constituencies and through them revives itself and grows.

Still, of course, there are those nasty extremists, and I would be naive if I did not recognize that they can be a trial to those who deal with them. But are the militant, alienated, ultras-of-the-left nothing more than foreign intruders? One quality of elite institutions, as opposed to ordinary institutions, is that they shape much more than they are shaped by the values of their members. It seems to me a distinct possibility that Berkeley has done something to create its problems, that the radicals are in some ways the progeny, as well as the prodigals, of their environment. And I suspect that Mr. Searle would accept this. For, if they were simply strangers in paradise, why would anyone try with such enthusiasm to make them feel more thoroughly at home?

I have another bone to pick with Mr. Searle's paper, and then I will concentrate on its virtues. In his theoretical section, he draws a distinction between what he calls the A.A.U.P.'s "special" conception of academic freedom, which he defines as limited to freedom in teaching and research, and his own "larger" conception, which he believes embodies the freedoms of the larger society. I think that distinction is misleading. The principles upheld by the A.A.U.P. have not merely been those that would safeguard teaching and research; they include, as I have pointed out in my paper, the civic or political freedoms of those who serve as teachers and researchers. In fact, far from settling for something less than the Constitution offers, the A.A.U.P. in effect presses for something more: it insists that the social penalties that may legally repay resented utterances—the loss of clients, the loss of job—shall not be inflicted upon professors. Of course, this all has to do with *professors*, and that is really the key. If the A.A.U.P.'s principles deserve to be labeled "minimalist" (I know a number of administrators who would not think so), it is not because they are narrowly constructed but because they are narrowly applied. If Mr. Searle's ideas deserve to be labeled "maximalist" (I myself would have some reservations about invoking ultimates), it is because they apply to the whole campus community, not because they import unfamiliar themes.

Nevertheless, I do believe that Mr. Searle has mapped out new and beguiling departures for dealing with student activists. To reduce the inconveniences under which they labor, he would have the university, through technical and other aids, assist in the staging of protest demonstrations. To turn leftist energies into constructive channels, he would give curricular recognition to some of the community projects they now support. I think these are more than peace-keeping strategies. What Berkeley seems to be trying to do is negotiate a new relationship with a radical, often disaffected, yet valuable student element, a relationship that may not only be mutually amicable but also educationally productive. With all the risks that this entails—and the risk of emasculating student radicalism by incorporation may be as great as the risk of seeming to conspire with it—the program, in my opinion, has a generous objective well worth its costs.

Mr. Searle does not take these costs lightly. Indeed, as he spoke of the hazards he is creating for the university, I wondered whether he was talking about an experiment or an explosive! And he has good reason to be apprehensive. The safest place to have launched such an innovation was surely not the University of California. By any prudential test, it should not have happened at a state university, which cannot collaborate with assaults on the public peace without hurting its chances at the public purse. Nor should it have happened in the state of California, where the presence of a powerful right makes any accommodation with the student left an occasion for furious comment. Probably, it should not have happened at any institution with so meddlesome a Board of Regents as that which rules at Berkeley. In short, this advance on the student-freedom front should have taken place at an institution like Columbia. But, as prudence does not dictate events, we are presented with an anomalous but far from unrewarding picture: an institution innovating under adverse circumstances, a vulnerable organization showing "guts."

■ DISCUSSION

J. SEARLE: I found myself agreeing with just about everything Mr. Metzger said. In fact, a lot of it I wish I had said myself. So I don't know to what extent he thinks he's in disagreement with me, but there are a couple of points. My talk was about a very specialized problem; the problem can be put in a rather crude political analogy. Last year we fought what has been described as a revolution. The problem of all revolutionaries is: When you win a revolution, where do you stop? How do you draw the line? Now I described analytically where I think we stopped the revolution, how far I want it to go. But the second problem of revolutionaries is: How do you stave off counterrevolution? And infantile left extremism? That is, in a kind of brutal political analogy, the problem I'm discussing. I'm trying to discuss that analytically in terms of the various forces that are in operation. When I discuss the moralizing and apocalyptic style of contemporary student radicalism I am not unmindful of such radicalizing forces in the world as racial injustice and the war in Viet Nam. The radical style does indeed have causes. But that does not alter the fact that it is a style profoundly alien to the spirit of academic inquiry, with its willingness to see the other point of view, its avoidance of the emotional and the *ad hominem*, and its cultivated hesitancy. The problem I am addressing myself to at present is not the justice of the radical goals but the consequences for the university of the radical means.

Now about "anti-intellectualism," or rather, as I more carefully expressed it, non-intellectualism. There *is* a certain attitude toward knowledge which informs my own approach, and I think most professional academics' approach, toward knowledge. It is the attitude that somehow or other knowledge really is a good thing in itself. The study of axiomatic set theory, for example, is a very exciting study. I don't know if it's useful for anything. I don't know that it's going to help us at all in solving any of the great social problems that I'm worried about, such as desegregation and peace, but I do nonetheless think axiomatic set theory and the foundations of mathematics are immensely worth studying just on their own account, because it's a good thing in itself to have knowledge and understanding. Now, when I characterize these groups as non-intellectual, what I'm saying is that, as intelligent as they are, they really don't accept that attitude to knowledge—that knowledge is a good thing in itself. A large percentage of them see knowledge primarily as a basis for action, and I think that this is a fundamentally different attitude from the one that universities traditionally are founded on.

I do not doubt the existence of the many students like Mr. Metzger's liberal intellectual pub companions. In fact, I regard them as a major part of the solution to the problem I am discussing. While they provide the infantry for campaigns mapped by a far more dedicated and single-minded student (and non-student) political leadership, they also provide a devastating veto power on the more irrational and unjustifiable decisions of that leadership, as we have found again and again at Berkeley. But their existence does not, as Mr. Metzger recognizes, remove the existence of what he calls the "nasty extremists." And the analytic problem is to understand that group, to understand it without hysteria, without sentimentality, and even without the patronizing irony of calling its members "nasty extremists."

■

D. COHEN: Mr. Searle's problem is that students and, to a lesser extent, faculty, characteristically have not, for various reasons, filled out the constitutional framework of liberty given in this country. And now they're beginning to try to do so. For whatever reason, they're students and faculty, and there they are in a university. But the problem of organizing to speak freely, to express one's political convictions in a society, cannot be restricted to a university. Quite plainly it's a public problem. And my feeling is that just so long as we confine our attention, in the way that the A.A.U.P. did, and expand it only beyond the guild to the apprentices, just so long shall we face an absolutely insoluble problem. We simply can't imagine student political activity or faculty political activity which is not relevant to the rest of society. Otherwise, you couldn't call it political, really, in the classical sense.

My own feeling is that probably, if there is to be real flesh put on the bones of liberty within the university, we might have to extend Mr. Metzger's historical logic and suggest that students and faculty who have live political concerns must reach out beyond the university, and not lay the entire burden of their political concerns and activity at the university's door. We should think about the whole society, about the problem of disenfranchisement and voicelessness in the society. That would yield a much broader description of reality, and perhaps a better comprehension of the problem of campus political activity. The problem is not simply that universities should legitimize students' concerns for what is real in their society. That to me isn't a problem; it's a good thing, and it's plainly happening in the universities because of what's been happening in the society— because of what students have been doing. To approach it in terms only of the university, however, would be to take a great deal of the sharpness and innovation out of what students and other people have been doing in America lately. The problem that such students, or such marginal student types have—the problem of people who come to a university, as someone said this morning, because they just can't think of any other place to go in this country—I think is a problem largely of the rhythm of learning.

This is a problem we owe mainly to the way in which American society makes its universities function. There are an awful lot of people in the universities who would rather postpone their learning for a while and go out and work in Mississippi or work in the prisons, or work somewhere else, or not do anything! Absorption or co-optation is no rational scheme for dealing with the vitality of the students at Berkeley or anywhere else. Rather, there is something wrong with a society where people cannot work out, in or out of school, the rhythm and pace of their own lives with some measure of decency. This is at the core of Mr. Goodman's critique of the culture. While the critique doesn't look like it in some respects, it is a profound structural critique. In many respects it is absolutely revolutionary. Therefore, to be consistent—or to try to be consistent—one has to go beyond the question of changing the university, or helping it to "accommodate" the students, and instead ask the question: What would it take to make the changes that this revolutionary critique of our culture and society involves? The changes would be revolutionary, and one of the characteristics of revolutionary changes is that it's very hard to persuade establishments to adopt them.

P. GOODMAN: Mr. Cohen made one remark which I think is an important one, when he spoke of the fact that this problem seems to have arisen precisely in the universities although it's really a general social problem. I don't think it's accidental. The chief issue in modern times, especially in terms of our discussion here (but it *is* a chief issue; that's why the discussion's a good one), is how under modern conditions to have substantive democracy as opposed to formal democracy. How, when the laws aren't really working, and the appeals to the President by mail aren't working, do you get them to pay attention? One of the ways is that you sit in, for instance. Now, it's obvious that that problem would especially arise among the excluded, those who are not in decision-making places, and the excluded in our society consist of displaced farmers who have so far been very silent, because they've given up economically; the aged, who manage to speak up and get their way, largely due to the Townsend movement; and the Negroes and the young. Remember that 48 per cent of the population is below twenty-six. And this group has no say. Going fifty years back—at fourteen most people went out to try to make a living and by eighteen they were not considered youths; they were young people. So we have a vast group of people who are really excluded. Now, in the Negroes and the young we find that there are very strong movements toward substantive democracy. I think you'd agree that this is an important reason why this issue has risen just among them, and we really have to have a social change which makes these excluded people not excluded from decision making. It's partly accidental that issues of academic freedom then come into the discussion.

■

I. LEVI: Mr. Searle has given us a very interesting account of the situation as he sees it at Berkeley; and he has some proposals and general outlines as to how some of the problems might be resolved. But he smuggles certain slogans into these proposals which deserve comment. For example, he wants to engage in a campaign outside of the academic community in the California legislature, presumably, among other things, to persuade them in some way that a university will not stand for any restrictions on the content of speech in a university. I may be in agreement with Mr. Searle that perhaps this is the stance one ought to take with the legislature. But what does "no restriction on content" mean if some student organization decides to engage in scurrilous comments about faculty members of a sort that can be seriously damaging, on an unwarranted basis, to a professor's reputation and position and status in some way *within* the academic community—not in a way that might conceivably be subject to the laws of libel, but within the academic community, given the structural context of the academic community? I believe—I hope I am right in supposing—that when Mr. Searle says there ought not to be any restrictions in content there is always some *ceteris paribus* clause in the background, because we cannot always anticipate beforehand the kinds of situation which will have to be covered by that specific slogan.

Here I sympathize with Mr. [S.] Kadish's point of view. Very often in his discussion Mr. Searle seems to agree. I have a sense, however, of some gaps between some of the proposals that Mr. Searle made about how to accommodate the alienated students at Berkeley into the academic environment and some of the slogans to which he referred. Of course, the slogans still may have some value even if they run the risk of being empty when qualified by *ceteris paribus*. But if that is true, then so do certain counter-slogans—for example, slogans which apparently are out of fashion at the moment. There does after all seem to me to be some sense in which it is a privilege for students to go to a university. I don't mean to suggest that all the mischief that has been done in the name of that slogan ought to be defended, but there are after all certain institutions of instruction, no matter what one may think of them, where I think the only way in a free society that we could defend having such institutions would be to say that students have a privilege to go there, even though severe restrictions are imposed upon their liberty. For example, in religious seminaries, it is clear that the very character of such institutions, if they are educational institutions, would be destroyed if they allowed the kinds of freedom for students that Mr. Searle wishes to advocate. At least I think those institutions would understand themselves as having their very character destroyed if this were true. Now, one proposal is to do away with such institutions. That, I submit, would be incompatible with the aims of a free society, of letting many flowers bloom. And it seems to me that this point about privilege does in some measure carry over to freer institutions of education, to universities of a non-sectarian character.

The reason I say this is apropos of Mr. Kadish's contrast between two conceptions of the objectives of the university. One is the university in its educational function, and one is the university in its function as a social critic. Those who advocate exploiting the university in its role as social critic want the university to be somehow or another a sanctuary for all kinds of criticism which can have some sort of effect, not simply within the confines of the university, but on society at large. It seems to me fair to take seriously the need for such institutions; however, in some sense those who are members of them are privileged in a way that other members of society are not, and as a consequence certain responsibilities are incumbent upon them. I am not here going to suggest any specific ways as to how these responsibilities are to be carried out. But it seems to me that it is one responsibility, of both faculty and students alike, not to impose severe censorship on what they say, but to induce a climate in the academic community in which discussion and criticism of whatever stripe, however radical, is carried on in terms of certain relatively high standards of intellectual responsibility. It seems to me that this slogan, that is, the slogan of responsibility to the debate, is one that ought not be neglected when we push a slogan like "no restriction on content." Now, an appeal to privilege, and appeal to responsibility, it seems to me, also have to be covered by a *ceteris paribus* clause, just as the appeal to the slogan "no restriction on content."

It seems to me that in many places the real problems are not in delineation of specific regulations regarding students' free speech but some concern with due process procedures which determine the content of *ceteris paribus* clauses. Administration and faculty have largely kept within their hip pockets, so to speak, decisions as to student behavior. Some of the issues regarding free speech don't seem to me to be centrally relevant, largely because the problems have not arisen in terms of which concrete proposals or sensible proposals can be made. What *is* lacking, I think, very often in universities at large is some sort of procedural machinery in terms of which these problems can be faced, and this seems to be the most central problem that can be universalized across the country, *not* the problem of thousands upon thousands of alienated students. I just don't see that. There are a few, maybe, around, but they do not, at least not here, seem to have that kind of influence upon the academic community.

P. GOODMAN: When Mr. Levi speaks of scurrilous language against professors, this has a terribly ominous ring of "good taste": "You see, we don't mind what the students say unless it is not in good taste." The canons of good taste of university administrators to me are so vulgar that I don't think they should be taken seriously. At the University of Wisconsin some years ago we had a problem of censorship of some poem that appeared in the literary magazine, and it was a beautiful poem and all the people who knew anything about poetry in the English Department were quite eager to see this poem in print, and defended it when action was taken against the student newspaper. But understandably, the provost of the university said he had no objection to free speech but of course it had to be in good taste, and the good taste was the taste of the worst boob in the community. That makes me very unhappy.

L. CROCKER: I think Mr. Goodman misinterpreted what Mr. Levi said about the matter of scurrilousness, etc. I think that Mr. Levi was *not* talking about good taste but rather about direct slander with injurious effects to a professor's life. Now, I happen to have seen this in a small Ohio institution where girls had the habit of standing in the professor's door and crying "rape," and there was no rape.

J. SEARLE: I've talked about these matters in front of other groups and I often get a response which I got today, and that is, "You don't really mean it! I mean, it sounds great but there's really that *ceteris paribus* clause; you know, the slogans are okay, but shucks, you don't really mean it!" Of course, in a formal sense every principle of behavior contains a *ceteris paribus* clause, because any principle can conflict with other principles. But that does not imply that we are not serious about free speech. I can assure you *we really mean it*—it's not a slogan! Now let me say what that means. That means if a student doesn't like the kind of lectures he's getting, he can and often does go out on the Sproul Hall plaza and deliver an analytical criticism, and it may or may not be scurrilous of the lectures that he heard, and there is, in fact, a book published every semester, called *The Slate Supplement to the General Catalog,* that makes savage criticisms of courses in the general catalog. And similarly with the point that Mr. Crocker raised, about the advocacy of illegal, off-campus activity. Yes, we *mean* it. That is, the criterion we employ in regulating campus activities is: Does it interfere with the normal functioning of the university? But, as long as speech is legal we permit it. That is, the act of advocacy is often legal where the act advocated is illegal, and even in cases where the act of advocacy is illegal, it's not the university that will proceed; we leave that to the courts. As far as our rules are concerned there's no restriction on advocating illegal off-campus activity. We're not talking about slogans here; we really are trying to experiment with this kind of freedom because we believe it has value in itself—and value for the university.

Well, Mr. Levi opposes to that another slogan, and the other slogan is intellectual responsibility. But I don't think these are opposite at all; rather I think the idea of freedom of speech, by which I mean no restriction on the content of speech, provides the form for discussion within the university; and *then* within the university one of the values that the university tries to infuse the students with is an ideal of intellectual responsibility, among all sorts of other values. I think he articulated subsequently a kind of fundamental assumption about the university that I think is wrong—and that is, that going to a university is a kind of privilege, and that, to put it in a slightly different way that I think he would accept, the university is basically a kind of a voluntary organization. Now maybe that's what it once was and maybe that's what it ought to be, but the brute facts about life in America today are that it's becoming an absolute necessity. It is difficult to lead a decent kind of a life in the United States without going through this university bit; and I quite agree, really, that since it is a very specialized institution, many of these people ought *not* to be here. Outside, of course, they'd be much happier, and the university would be able to proceed more smoothly. Then, I think, as they got older they might see certain values in the university and be ready to come to the university, but that's not one of the live options available to us. The way the system is set now it is not a voluntary organization; it's a kind of necessary phase in the lives of millions of young people, and that's the assumption that we operate on, that we have to cope with.

That brings up the questions raised by Mr. Cohen. He says, "Well, are we really worried about society in general and the changes that are going on in America?" Of course we are. All of this that we're talking about is against that background. But, at the same time, we have to run a university, we have to preserve the values of a university and the freedom that a university is supposed to be guaranteeing in a society that is going through these really fundamental, revolutionary changes. Let me say one or two points about them. There's a revolution going on in America that we don't really understand and there are all sorts of different aspects to it; the civil rights revolution is part of it, but, for example, there's a kind of sexual revolution that's going on as well. All sorts of attitudes towards society and the goals of society are being revolutionized. Calvin Coolidge could say, "The business of America is business," and everybody thought that was wonderful; they elected him President! Nobody would have the nerve to make a remark like that today. There's a kind of crisis of confidence in the American establishment. It's not clear where the kind of basic liberal assumptions we have relied on are getting us: maybe that wasn't the right way to approach civil rights; maybe that's *really* what's getting us into this Vietnam mess. Well-intentioned guys proceeding on a set of half-articulated, really un-articulated, assumptions they don't understand. And *all* that we've been talking about in universities is going on against these very subtle but very profound changes —these changes that I think can accurately be described as a kind of crisis in American life.

That leads me to my last point, which is really that, if we can't cope with these kinds of changes in the university, then we can't cope with them at all. That is, the university assumes a kind of special responsibility in an era of this type. At the same time that it's under these terrific pressures, it has a responsibility to try to preserve certain kinds of values and give content to the ideals of freedom which the general society gives lip service to but, because of various technological reasons and organizational and societal reasons, is not really giving adequate content to. One last point. Mr. Levi suggested that really the young people of today aren't so alienated as I have indicated—just a few people on the West Coast. I would like to respond to that (and really this is just a kind of guess because I don't have any more data than he does). My feeling is we haven't *begun* to understand the depths of the alienation—that we're shortly going to be faced with a situation in this country where more than half of the population is under twenty-five, and many of them have absolutely no feeling of belonging to what some people call the "power structure." Now, you want to talk about alienation; we are really headed for a very serious situation in this country, arising out of the kind of alienation that you can detect. Look at the changes in adolescent culture. For example, Bobby Dylan would have been inconceivable for the high school generation and the college generation that I grew up in, but now what are the figures—I mean, is it one in every ten students actually owns a Bobby Dylan record? This is a staggering statistic. I cite it as one of many random bits of apparently inconsequential data, but I really think they add up to something.

s. KADISH: I have just a few comments, mainly suggested by Mr. Searle's last remarks. I think there's a good deal in what he says that shakes you up, but sometimes I have the feeling that maybe it's not that bad. When you don't know how to swim and you're in six feet of water and you're floundering around, it seems like an ocean with bottomless depths. It may be that because we're in the middle of something that's hard for one to understand and unravel it seems very deep, profound, very portentous and near doomsday. But it may not be. Don't misunderstand me; it may be, but it may *not* be! We had all kinds of incredible, adolescent, puerile occupations when I was a kid, too. They weren't quite so political, although some were, but I remember vividly how my elders would shake their heads and stroke their beards and worry what was happening to the younger generation. I think we can romanticize our own problems a little bit. It gives us, somehow, not only a feeling of dread and apprehension, but also somehow it's kind of satisfying to our egos to view our position as in the center of a maelstrom. I don't want to put it off as just the trivial outpourings of a wild bunch of kids. Really, I take it seriously. Whether it is a torrent of history or something less significant, I frankly don't know. It may well be we are experiencing with this generation something comparable in magnitude to the way in which modern methods of destruction have changed the whole concept of war. War and peace and stability and international relations have always been problems since government started; now we come to something different all of a sudden—it's the atomic bomb. (I'm not even sure, by the way, that in terms of the pervasive problems of man's viability on this earth, the atomic bomb raises problems that weren't faced many times throughout history.)

All I meant to suggest with regard to each generation's self-concern was that it may be good to have a little humility in the face of the times—perhaps the tide seems bigger because it bothers us more. Maybe in terms of its magnitude and what it portends it's not so different in quality from what we faced earlier. I'm not suggesting that is so; I'm suggesting it as a very plausible hypothesis. I'm suggesting that people tend to over-exaggerate their illness; you know, *my* sickness seems worse than anybody else's sickness because it's *mine*. I don't know how anyone can demonstrate that you are right in your view or I am right in mine. Probably we'll find out, perhaps in our lifetime. I don't know. I think, anyway, we're more apt to act quietly and rationally if we act with a little more detachment and more sense of history. All of these things have histories; they have roots, they go back; other people in other times struggled with life's problems—yes, even with rebellious students and youthful malaise. Maybe we can learn some wisdom, if not from intelli-gent past ways of responding, then from the fact that in time one seemingly overarching problem gave way to others in turn.

Another comment I want to make. I'm very grateful to my friend Ike Levi for giving me a good phrase. The famous December 8 resolution that Mr. Searle talked about was a very important resolution in which it was stated that there may be restrictions on the time, place, and manner with regard to political utterance, but none whatsoever on the content of speech. Now I want to tell you that I voted for that! I voted for that heartily but with a certain reservation and a certain feeling of doubt and I know now the phrase I could have invoked to satisfy myself: "I vote aye—*ceteris paribus!*"

Mr. Searle knows more about what the prevailing rules are at the university right now; he's pretty largely responsible for making them, and if he says right now there is no restriction on content, it's okay. But there's another issue that I'd like to say a word about. How long will that be? I know how long Mr. Searle is going to be in the administration; it isn't going to be very long if he has anything to do with it. But the question is, how long will that be and how long should it be and can you justly and fairly deny certain kinds of restrictions, really, on content. Let me just give you a few examples which give me that *ceteris paribus* feeling. I give you obscenity. I give you not just the timid kind of obscenity you read in books—that's fine—but I give you someone standing up in front of a large crowd and using the most vulgar four-letter epithets you ever heard. Now, if you restrict, if you say no, if you discipline, I submit to you that's a restriction on content! It's not time, it's not place, it's not manner—whether you do it in a loud or a small voice—it is content. And there's a case for restricting obscenity of this kind. There's a case against it; but there's a case for it! Likewise, do you know what a conspiracy is? A conspiracy is an agreement, and you make agreements typically by the exchange of words. Now, I would think that if a couple of students got together and made a deal directed to cheating on an examination and this was all done through the form of words—it never got off the ground, it didn't succeed—the university might legitimately impose some kind of protective discipline in order to protect the system. It would be a restriction on content. Or I give you the *Slate Supplement* that Mr. Searle referred to—a very useful, great document. It shakes up the faculty; they wait apprehensively for its appearance and take it with them into dark corners of the university to read. But suppose that *Slate Supplement* was corrupt? Suppose it was bought out? Suppose that what you read there are carefully selected pay-offs for certain professors or certain interests? I submit that it would be a legitimate university function to see what's going on, to straighten out the truth, to clamp down in some discreet way upon that kind of activity. Again content! Or I give you the case we talked about: the advocacy, and the organization which Mr. Searle very perspicaciously points out is usually implicit in advocacy of criminal acts to take place on the campus or off the campus. The mere fact that it is a crime independently to organize for a criminal enterprise, and therefore that the general criminal sanction of the community may be invoked, does not disentitle the university from itself imposing some kind of protective discipline—to prevent students using its resources from carrying out on the campus this crime of conspiracy, for which in a real sense it may justly be held accountable.

■

J. SEARLE: The whole basis of my remarks this morning was that you ought to give them [students engaged in certain off-campus projects] credit. That doesn't mean you've got to abandon your intellectual standards altogether. You have to have pretty tight control, I think, over the intellectual content of these programs. You can't have the situation where just *anything* gets credit. Phillips Brooks House at Harvard, which is a big operation of this kind, is extracurricular activity—it's not, as I understand it, part of the academic program. I'm proposing this now as part of the academic program. Now, we do have this as extracurricular activities on a smaller scale.

P. GOODMAN: One of the projects they were interested in in the free university at Berkeley last spring was the organization of migrant labor in the California plantations. Do you really think the state of California would take kindly to this one? How can you then tell the students that this one is academically respectable and that one is not?

J. SEARLE: You don't tell them that. You say that the state will let us do this one and it won't let us do that one. You tell them the truth. Some other examples. There's a good program working now with drug addiction in San Francisco. It's called Synanon and it's very controversial because it involves a completely different attitude to drug addicts and it involves group therapy. It makes the community nervous. And the people in these towns get nervous if they think desegregating housing is going to affect property values, and so on. This is the sort of thing that makes them very upset. But I just want to say something in response to Professor Levi, who felt that this wouldn't really satisfy the activist urges. The number of people that we have volunteering for these programs is just extraordinary. The word goes out that you can go to work with Synanon and two hundred people sign up just like that. The urge to do this just amazes me—the number of people. Now, true, you do get certain problems. For example, we sent some students to Oakland—this is extracurricular—to teach people how to read. We discovered some of them were trying to make revolutionaries; they weren't teaching how to read at all! They were saying, "You've got to understand about the power structure and what we've got to do," and this is the sort of thing that suggests to me that we have to have fairly close supervision, *if* you're going to offer academic credit for it.

I. LEVI: Mr. Searle's last remark reflects some of the lack of comfort I have. He sounds like a man who wants to be outside of the establishment but really wants to be with it. I really don't know because I don't know the radically alienated students he describes. But given Mr. Searle's description of the students and the quality of their alienation, I cannot imagine that a serious program of good works within the university would accommodate the problem as he posed it this morning. Maybe his initial description was misleading to me; maybe the situation did not as radically involve so profound a rebellion on the part of the students as he described, but if it does, it seems to me that at best such good-works programs will be a temporary palliative until the students get the idea of what's being done to them.

P. GOODMAN: I think the insinuation that the radical students object to the institutionalization is quite wrong, because they institutionalize themselves beautifully. I think what they object to is when the institution becomes unauthentic and when, in fact, the good-works program proves to be a sell-out of the people that they're working with. Now, in regard to the reading program, when we were doing it in New York with the Northern Student Movement, the students who were working with the Northern Student Movement soon found out that teaching reading meant making the kids not want to succeed in public school, and the aim of the program originally had been to upgrade them in the public schools. Therefore the Northern Student Movement said, "Let's forget the public school and really teach these kids something." Now, you might call this teaching revolutionary. I would think it's real education.

J. SEARLE: I wanted to say something about why I think that this kind of thing is so deeply satisfying precisely for the alienated student, and that is that he makes a difference. One of the great frustrations that people with liberal views in America have is that they feel they're not making any difference, but the extraordinary range of types of political activists who are now engaged in this kind of community service, and the things they have to say about it, suggest to me that they *do* find it deeply satisfying. The same way with Peace Corps people; incidentally, Berkeley sends more people to the Peace Corps than any other campus in the country, so it isn't that they're dismayed with the Peace

Corps. The satisfaction that these people get is that it really makes a difference—they are really doing something.

I. LEVI: I have no doubt that many students will take to such programs enthusiastically. But it seems to me that such students are not so utterly alienated from the university and the society in which they live as those that Mr. Searle described.

■

Mr. Searle seems to assume that somehow or another we have to think in terms of a set of rules which will anticipate all situations, and if we can't do that, then what we have to mean by "no restriction on content" is, by gum, no restriction on content—no *ceteris paribus* clause, no reservation that will have to be worked out. The crucial thing, I think, when you do introduce the *ceteris paribus* clause, is the process in terms of which this is interpreted. Some procedure is required to interpret the *ceteris paribus* clause by having a certain kind of institutional machinery that will seem non-arbitrary to all the parts, students or faculty or administration, in terms of which one can hammer out when the case arises the specific details of the *ceteris paribus* clause for the case at hand. It seems to me that a good deal of worry goes into laying down certain general principles—what students may do and what students may not do—when the real source of student grievances ought to be the lack of access, the relative arbitrariness with which university law, if it can be called that, is administered and decided and legislated from their point of view. In short, what we really ought to be worrying about, I think, is *that* kind of institutional reform within the university.

J. SEARLE: I don't know how anybody could get the idea that I thought you ought to try and work out rules and anticipate everything in advance. That's precisely the reverse of what I've been saying all the time, that if you imagine all these bizarre and extreme counter-examples and try to legislate for them, if anything you tend to aggravate the situation. What you should do, as I've been saying over and over, is be as little doctrinaire as possible; and by that I mean even the liberal doctrinaire line is inadequate to describe the problems of the present situation.

What we've got to do is decide what our objectives are and work toward those objectives in a very piecemeal fashion. We don't have the rules in our hip pockets. Our rules situation is pretty complicated. There are the Regents' policies and underneath them the campus rules. Now what we're trying to do is set up a representative mechanism; this is where the democratic stuff comes in; we're trying to set up a mechanism whereby the students and the faculty will have a representative committee to make rules. About due process, the fact of the matter is we haven't really got it worked out and I think we're in for a long period of experimentation. On first sight it sounds like, "Well, in the university you ought to have everything they have in a court!" But that really is impractical. It just won't work. It takes forever and by the time you get ready to suspend a student he's long since graduated. Students like this idea, incidentally. But you don't have the powers of a court. You can't find anybody in contempt of court; you can't subpeona a witness, and so on. There are so many different kinds of due process—the concept we're really looking for is a concept of a fair hearing and that means confrontation of witnesses and the right of the accused to have a written presentation of the charges, and so on. So the answer about rules and due process at Berkeley is that we're trying to put the campus rules as far as possible in the hands of the people who will be governed by those rules, and about due process, we're experimenting with ways of giving some reality to the notion of a fair hearing on campus.

W. METZGER: As your East Coast representative I might report to you that until recently my institution had the most rudimentary conception of academic due process and that even now its rules on dismissal procedures leave much to be desired. The basic legislation on this subject was passed at Columbia in 1917, to meet the exigencies of the First World War. It has remained marvelously suited to that purpose ever since! Of course, it goes without saying that the character of the rules does not depict the conscience of the institution. Columbia behaves much better than most of its edicts say it has to.

IV

ESSAY: Sanford H. Kadish

REPLY: Paul Goodman

DISCUSSION

IV

□ Essay: SANFORD H. KADISH

The terms of reference of this discussion are freedom and order, and the focus is the university. I understand these terms to suggest the tension produced between the highly valued interests of self-determination and the demands of social living. In a word, social restraint becomes a kind of necessary evil that serves to carry the social venture forward. Now, social restraints obviously are of many kinds. There are formal kinds in the form of rules; there are informal kinds in the form of customs and expectations; there are positive kinds of restraints and negative kinds of restraints; there are spontaneous ones and there are deliberate ones. And all of these restraints, operating together, create a kind of order which makes it possible for social communities to operate.

As a lawyer I'm primarily concerned about, and am therefore going to talk about, one kind of social restraint. I want to make clear that I'm aware that it is only one kind of restraint, and that the operation of social communities requires all these others as well. The restraint with which I am concerned is that produced by rules and their enforcement—in other words, by deliberate, prospective, authoritative definitions of socially prohibited conduct, and the imposition of sanctions, that is to say, undesired consequences, upon violators of those norms as a means of achieving a general conformity with them. I want to talk, first of all, generally about rules and their enforcement apart from the context of the university community; then I want to apply some of those general observations to the problem of fashioning rules and creating conformity to those rules by the use of sanctions within the university.

Rules and sanctions as I've defined them obviously serve the interest of order in the community. This is their most obvious characteristic. I want to suggest that they also have a benign side, that the fashioning of rules and sanctions also serves the interest of freedom, by imposing limitations upon the exercise of discretion by the holders of authority. Moreover, the process of formulating rules also can serve the interests of freedom by providing the opportunity and the occasion to test and challenge the legitimacy of particular social restraints and their application on particular occasions. It makes possible constant re-examination of what kinds of social restraints we want and what kinds are legitimate.

The criminal code exemplifies these two sides of rules and sanctions—the restraint side and the freedom side. On the one hand, the criminal code is a compendium of criminal conduct, of course, but at the same time, and this is most important, a criminal code is also an exclusion of conduct, that is to say, a protection of conduct which is not prohibited and which therefore may not be visited with a criminal sanction. There's been an effort in the last ten years to produce something which we call a Model Penal Code, an attempt to put together what a sound and rational body of substantive criminal law should look like. The code attempts to set down in the first section the purposes of a penal code. Let me read you four of the five chief functions it sets up for a criminal code. I do this to exemplify the general point I'm making about rules. "The general purposes," it says, "of the provisions governing the definition of offenses are: (a) to forbid and prevent conduct that unjustifiably and inexcusably inflicts or threatens substantial harm to individual or public interests; . . . (c) to safeguard conduct that is without fault from condemnation as criminal; (d) to give fair warning of the nature of the conduct declared to constitute an offense; (e) to differentiate on reasonable grounds between serious and minor offenses."

Viewing the substantive criminal law in this way draws attention to a number of critical issues in the fashioning of rules. First, what kind of conduct may and what kind of conduct may not be legitimately coerced by the threat of the criminal sanction? Second, what mode of communication should we use in announcing the conduct which is prohibited in order to maximize the interest of self-determination? That is to say, how should we meet the need for specificity of language in order to avoid a retroactive application of the law and to preclude vesting the courts with too great an authority to define the criminal law themselves in the process of enforcing it? This is the principle of legality. Third is the issue of procedure, of devising the means and processes for applying the sanction to alleged violators in a way which comports with interests of fairness and preserves a general sense of security—due process of law, in short. Inform a person, apprise him, allow him to confront his accusers, provide him with an unprejudiced tribunal—these kinds of factors. Fourth is the issue of measuring sanctions for violations, in order to economize on the use of force upon the individual; it is the notion of proportionality of punishment.

I don't mean to suggest that the benign, protective side of rules and their enforcement (represented in these four issues) is always present. Certainly, it is not present in authoritarian political systems. And even in democratic ones like ours, it is unevenly in evidence. For example, while our criminal law is a classic case where these benign principles operate, as I tried to suggest, there are, even within the criminal process, areas which are largely untouched by concern for the principles of legality and due process of law and the proportionality of punishment.

Now, what kinds of factors tend to inhibit the development of the benign side of a system of rules is a very important and open question. Sometimes, the factors are expressed in dogmatic terms. For example, it is said that where the state is only offering a privilege or a benefit to a suppliant, it may do so on any terms and through whatever modes it deems desirable. Sometimes the considerations for denying these benign attributes of rules and sanctions is a pragmatic one, an instrumental one. That is to say, we need the flexibility that comes with free discretion; we can't bind our hands with legalistic rules which tend just to rigidify the system—we've got to keep flexible and open, so that we have maximum room to meet new kinds of situations.

I think all of these considerations are apparent in the debate over the governance of the student body in the public university, to which I now want to turn.

Traditionally, the government of students has been marked by the restraint dimension of rules and sanctions, that is to say, by "rules undomesticated." Some examples of this are suggested in Mr. Metzger's remarks. Let me try one or two others. A decision of the Kentucky Supreme Court in 1913 observed that "College authorities stand *in loco parentis* concerning the physical and moral welfare, and mental training of the pupils, and we are unable to see why, to that end, they may not make any rules or regulations for the government or betterment of the pupils that a parent could for the same purpose." A New York court observed in 1928: "The university reserves the right and the student concedes to the university the right to require the withdrawal of any student at any time for any reason deemed sufficient to it, and no reason for requiring such withdrawal need be given." Especially since the Second World War, however, the benign, "freedom" dimension of rules has begun to make its appearance with great dramatic force. One sees this in student and faculty demands, in new codes of student behavior and discipline (the University of Oregon code, for example, is a model of legality and due process), in the kinds of judicial decisions that Walter Metzger was referring to, in constitutional decisions, in the literature of debate, and even, alas, in student demonstrations. I think this trend is unmistakable. It's a healthy and desirable trend, and I think it will continue. But as it does we will be confronted by the challenging task of determining what kinds of limitations are appropriate upon the exercise of authority through rules, given the special needs and functions of the university community. This will entail facing the kinds of questions which I suggested earlier are exemplified in the formulation of the criminal code.

First, what kinds of student conduct should be prohibited and what kinds should be left free? What kind should be left to the civil authorities and what dealt with by the university authorities?

Second, how precisely need the rules be formulated? Need they be formulated with the precision of a tax code? With the care of a penal code? Is it enough that they look like administrative regulations? May they take the form of a kind of golden rule—"Do unto others"—is that enough?

Third, how should the rules be enforced? What procedures are desirable to determine whether a student has violated the rules? Do we need a "trial-type" hearing which looks like a criminal trial? Will a lesser degree of formality suffice for the purpose? Do you need to assure the right to counsel to students who are up for discipline? If they don't have lawyers do you have to appoint lawyers for them? Should we allow cross-examination or should we not? Does it depend on what the alleged infraction is? Who should bring the charges? Deans? Professors? The student body representative? Who should be the prosecutor? How much discretion should he have? Who should hear and determine? Should it be the students themselves? Which students? How should they be selected? Should it be the administrators? Should it be—God forbid!—the faculty who would be obliged to hear and determine these matters? At Berkeley, for example, an experiment being considered is the use of hearing examiners in the shape of dragooned members of the faculty, probably, to my dismay, from the law school.

Fourth, what should be the range of sanctions and what sanctions should be used for what violations? We're pretty rigid; we don't have very many tricks in our bag. We kick a kid out or we let him stay in; we put him on probation, whatever that means, or we suspend him for a term. What other kinds of sanctions of the more flexible, versatile character can be devised which are appropriate to the occasion?

Fifth, underlying all of those issues: Who should make the judgments in each of these four categories? Who should be the government? How should the authority to make resolutions of those issues be distributed among the student body, the faculty, and even, if I dare say so, the administrators?

Now obviously, it is not feasible here to deal with all five of those issues, and I think anyway it would be pointless. Ultimately the answers will be forged over the years; they will not be given dogmatically from on high. Not even from the height of the lecture podium. They will be forged by pressures within the academic community, by external community pressures, by students, by decisions of law courts, by writing, by experiments. And the answers will come, I think, piece by piece, one at a time, pragmatically, rather than by any kind of programmatic prescription, and I think that is to the good.

I want to use my remaining time to talk about only one of those classes of questions, the first one mentioned: What kinds of student conduct should be prohibited and what left free? What left to civil authorities and what dealt with by the university authorities? And, if it's fair game so to limit my target, I want to address myself to only one kind of conduct; namely, that which generally falls within the area of political and social expression. This has given rise to the most thought and has been most contentiously debated, at least where I come from. How might one rationally approach determining which, if any, of this conduct is properly reachable by university rule and sanction?

I think the essential task in defining conduct that is appropriate for rule making, and distinguishing it from conduct that is not, is to determine the existence of a legitimate regulatory interest or concern by the university. That needs a little amplification. As an example, to take a clear case, the university has no legitimate regulatory concern in whether the students are dutiful and courteous to their parents on their holidays. But, at the other extreme, it *does* have a legitimate, regulatory interest in whether or not the students cheat on examinations. Now most of us agree that this is so. But why? I suggest that you make a judgment about the end which would be served by such rules and judge whether or not the university has a concern or interest in achieving those ends, given what we regard as the proper functions and purposes of the university. Now, I think in order to make this judgment it isn't always necessary to agree on a kind of *Weltbild*, a glorious picture, a final delineation of the function and purposes of the university. Often, it is enough simply to judge more narrowly that the end sought by the particular rule is consistent with no possible function that the university may legitimately claim, although I grant you that sometimes one will have to get down to brass tacks and have it out on the final issue of what a university should be.

In a moment I want to look at five or six kinds of particular situations within the area of political activity to which I will try to suggest how one might apply this tool of regulatory interest. But first, I want to make two observations about university interests in general. First of all, as I look at the problem of governing a student body in the university, there are two predominant kinds of regulatory concern. The first is the concern which is directly produced by the internal needs and functioning of the university as a center for teaching, training, and research. The other interest or concern is directly produced by relationships between the university and the larger community in which it functions—diplomatic concerns or interests, if you will.

The second observation I want to make concerns different views one might have of the university function. I think that here, in the area of political activity, how you come out is going to depend as usual on how you go in, and where you go in in this context means, what relationship do you see as proper between political activity by students and the functions of a university? Let me give you just two different ones.

In a speech in March of 1965, Acting Chancellor Myerson observed as follows:

> Free political discussion should . . . be encouraged on university campuses because it furthers the educational process, not because it may contribute to social reform. Indeed, all activities other than scholarship and learning which go on on a campus must be viewed as secondary to the main university objectives: this applies as much to baseball as to politics, as much to fraternities as to the Associated Students of the University of California. Should any secondary activity tend to receive more than secondary attention, the university is not only justified but obligated to place that activity in proper perspective, possibly through some kind of a rationing device.

Now that's one view: Politics is secondary. Its justification is only educational. The university has no direct concern with social reform. Politics must be kept in its proper secondary place.

An opposite view looks upon the function of a university as primarily social criticism. It has been ably described by my colleague, Dr. Lunsford, in an unpublished study. The major purpose of a university in a free society is criticism of society for its own improvement. This means more than the provision of a marketplace for ideas. It means more than a haven for academic research by faculty of certified competence. According to this view, to quote Dr. Lunsford,

> Any university worth its keep must create dissatisfaction with society in the very process of helping students to think independently. It does this when it makes them aware of men's aspirations throughout history, and when it sharpens their intellectual capacities to distinguish practice and principle, deeds and promises, consistency and contradiction. Where students progress through higher learning complacently acceptive of society as they find it, so the argument runs, just there has the university failed of its highest purpose.

Consequently, the university should be the conscience of the community, the seedbed of dissent where the worst departures between the ideals and the realities of the community can be pointed out and criticized. This is the prime function of the university. I'd like you to have before you those two views of the relationship between politics and the university, and my suggestion of the division of concerns of interest into internal and external categories. With this in mind let us get down to cases, and raise questions concerning a number of kinds of situations in which it is arguable whether or not rules are legitimate.

Let me start with the least arguable kind of case: namely, those kinds of restrictions which are designed to keep political activity from interfering with itself and other activities—so-called "time, place, and manner" restrictions which everybody, at least on the Berkeley campus, seems agreed are legitimate and justifiable. That is to say, you can talk in certain places at certain times although not too loudly. You can't festoon the whole campus with giant billboards and sexy signs; you've got to conform to some kinds of restrictions in the interests of the use of the university by others. It's very obvious what I'm talking about here. I suppose also with time, place, and manner restrictions properly ought to go those which confine the university's facilities and resources to the people it's designed to serve, the student body and the faculty. And I suppose that the concern or interest which justifies restrictions of this kind, even though they are restrictions upon the free exercise of political activity, no matter how you slice it, is that they are needed to prevent interference with other people's political and related activities, and to assure some kind of an even sharing of resources and opportunities. Now, I think there would be broad agreement on this. But when you get beyond time, place, and manner restrictions it gets more difficult and more debatable. I want to present an array of situations which I think very broadly move out from the more justifiable to the less justifiable; that is, I will start with a situation where I think you can make a strong case for restriction and then move out to situations where the case for the restriction becomes harder to justify.

Let me next raise the issue, therefore, of restrictions on the obscene and the offensive. We had a share of that at Berkeley. What I'm talking about is the use of language in our community which is regarded as violently offensive to one's sensibility. It's not just indelicate; it's felt to be ugly and vulgar. Now those are emotion-laden words. This is the way the words are taken in our community. Does the university have any concern or interest consistent with its function in putting boundaries on the use of such language? That's the issue. Now I suppose if a student in class got up on his feet and responded to a professor with the kind of language I'm talking about—the classic four-letter-word obscenity—a professor would be justified in putting him out of the classroom at the very least. I presume I would get no argument on that—this would be conduct directly disruptive of the educational process, demeaning of the processes of intellectual exchange. Is there any like concern on the part of the university in maintaining similar levels of discourse in extramural, open public addresses on the squares of the campus? I find it difficult to say that there is no legitimate interest in preventing the processes of open exchange from being impaired by the gratuitous public use of words people find grossly assaultive and offensive. Nonetheless, I have the gravest problem with regulations of this kind because of the difficulty in determining what's obscene and what isn't. This is one of the most difficult kinds of problem. Surely the community at large has this same interest in preventing obscenity, but you know for yourselves the kinds of gross invasions into freedom of speech and freedom of the arts that the enforcement of obscenity laws poses. But it must be emphasized that we are talking here about the way in which ideas are communicated: the wires of communication. I would think that the university has a special obligation to keep them working, to maintain their effectiveness—not to interfere with them but to maintain them. Please remember that I am speaking about this one kind of *assaultive* obscenity, the kind that is shouted from the platform, to be heard whether you like it or not, not the kind that is read in a book.

Now to move to another kind of situation: conduct engaged in by students while on the campus which is a crime under the law of the state. Does this suffice to justify the university in imposing its own independent sanction upon such students? For example, an active conspiracy among a bunch of students on the campus of the university to blow up an arms depot in the nearby area in order to prevent its use for the Viet Nam war. Now, no doubt the students could be subjected to criminal penalties; they've committed the crime of conspiracy. The question is: What is the proper stance for the university to assume over these students in this situation? I would suggest that the mere fact that the conduct is committed by students on the campus—that mere fact alone without more—is not enough to justify the university in imposing its sanction. After all, in the example I've given and all others like it, it's the community's laws and interests that are injured. The community therefore has a legitimate concern, a stake in applying the criminal sanction to this kind of conduct. The university, in the instance I give you, is *not* responsible as a collaborator or an accomplice; it is not implicated just because the wrongdoers happen to be students who happen to engage in their conspiratorial activities while they are on campus. No offense against *it* has been committed.

Is the same true of all kinds of crimes? Does the fact that the students' conduct on the campus constitutes a crime under the laws of the state mean that the university has no business imposing its own discipline? I would think plainly not. There are certain kinds of conduct designated as criminal under the laws of the general community which the university community *would* have a legitimate interest or concern in preventing. For example, breaking into my office and stealing the examination questions is burglary. The fact that it's burglary and that the student may be criminally punished does not of itself disentitle the university from imposing its own sanction upon the conduct, because it has an *independent* concern, independent of that of the general community. What I am suggesting, in short, is that the mere fact of criminality occurring within the campus boundaries is not decisive one way or another on whether or not the university may regulate conduct through the use of its own rules and sanctions.

Now we move to the next situation, a very ticklish one. It has to do with restrictions on on-campus staging of off-campus criminal activities. Let me give you an example here. Suppose a large number of students, making use of university facilities and microphones, and operating under a kind of license from the university to set up tables and gather an audience, set about urging all of the people there to construct wooden crosses, soak them in kerosene and march out into the surrounding community and plant burning crosses on the lawns of Jewish citizens. This all takes place openly, before the university authorities. Has the university any business doing anything? Has it any legitimate interest or regulatory concern in view of its function? Take another case, because we must take both of these cases together. Take a large body of students who similarly organize and advocate, through the exploitation of similar university-provided facilities, a plan to lie down on the tracks in front of troop trains as a gesture of protest against the Viet Nam war. It happens to be a crime to do that, just as it happens to be a crime to plant crosses and burn them on the lawns of citizens. And it happens to be criminal to conspire and incite to the commission of these crimes. And those who do so will be just as guilty as those who actually do the acts—in the law we would call them accomplices. What kind of legitimate regulatory interest does the university have? Is it any business of the university? Is it justified in making rules to prevent such use of its locale and its facilities and to sanction their violation? I would think, with John Searle, that the answer is surely yes. For the university otherwise becomes a kind of accomplice itself in the criminal activities, in its knowing toleration of the use of its instruments and facilities to commit criminal acts. Now I'm suggesting that's the end of the matter. The sanctioned conduct involves speech, and in a political context. The gravest problems of undue interference with freedom of speech threaten, if the rules are not drawn with scrupulous specificity and narrowly confined, and if procedures for determining the crucial facts are not impeccably fair. Indeed, there are dangers even so, and there is much to be said for a university which resists applying its sanctions in these cases unless they are gross. But all I am asserting is that it is dogmatic foolishness to insist that this is no business of the university and that the university must turn its back.

In the previous two situations students engaged in criminal activities on the campus. And what seems to me crucial was that the university was not itself involved in the first case, but it was inevitably involved in the second, where its facilities and instruments were being openly exploited to the knowledge of the university and everyone else. Now consider another situation. Here again students engage in criminal activities, but this time the conduct takes place off the campus and the only nexus between the university and the conduct is that it is students who are engaging in the conduct. For example, a student commits a jailable misdemeanor in driving his car; a student riots with others in the streets or sits in on the premises of a newspaper with whose policies he disagrees; a student commits assault and battery in a barroom brawl; a student embezzles funds from an off-campus organization; a student deliberately burns his draft card—a federal offense; a student is apprehended selling narcotics; a student sexually molests a minor. What generalizations about the legitimate regulatory concern of the university can one make in the face of this wide variety of types of conduct, all of which are criminal?

In medieval universities students gained an immunity from criminal accountability to the outside community; they had a kind of sanctuary because they were in the university. The university itself, therefore, maintained responsibility for discipline of its members. Today, of course, we have nothing like that. Nonetheless, the university in some situations may seek (many have done so) to protect a student against the severity of a criminal prosecution by venturing to handle the matter itself, even though this might entail some kind of discipline. The interest here is protective. I think few people would protest university intervention of this kind, although it does partake of guardianship and perhaps I underestimate the vigor with which some would insist on extirpating all remnants of the *parens patrie* role of the university.

The foregoing aside, I suggest that the mere fact that the person committing a crime is a student gives the university no justification for imposing its own discipline. The private life of a student is his own affair; the non-university-connected conduct of a student is not the affair of the university. And this seems to me true whether or not the student has been prosecuted and convicted. If he has not, it is not for the university to substitute its adjudicatory procedures for those of the criminal law. If he has, it is not for the university to add its own punishment to that imposed (or withheld) by the criminal-law authorities.

But is this true of all conduct which is criminal? Not necessarily. What I mean to suggest is that it is not the criminality of the student's conduct that creates the university concern; it is the nature of the conduct. That a student drives his car recklessly, or carries his sense of righteousness to the point of burning his draft card or committing criminal trespass, is not the business of the university. If it is, its interest is in furthering the humanizing processes of education unabated. But a student who pushes dope? Who is sexually assaultive? Here the university has an interest in protecting the whole university community against dangers which particular students may have shown themselves to constitute. I won't carry the matter further. Obviously the task of making judgments in particular cases will be difficult. But I believe the lines I've suggested are the ones which should be pursued in making the judgments. The final two situations I had in mind raising were (1) restrictions on political and social action on the campus (electioneering, recruitment, solicitation) and (2) restrictions on invited speakers. Let me just say quickly, and hence dogmatically, that the proper interests of the university seem to me to require encouragement, or at the very least a hands-off policy, here, rather than the imposing of restrictions based upon the views of its Establishment about what political activities students should engage in or what speakers students should invite to speak to them. This is now the policy of Berkeley and I trust it will eventually be the policy of universities everywhere.

If there is one theme in all my remarks it is this: The awakening of unrest and protest concerning university rules for governing students does not signify the ending of rules and sanctioning. Communities must be governed if they are to survive as communities. It signifies rather the ending of arbitrary and ungoverned assertion of authority and the beginning of law in its best sense—ordered controls, articulated deliberatively and with restraint, and both formulated and applied in ways calculated to enlarge the ambit of freedom. In a word, the principle of legality is about to matriculate into university government.

■ Reply: PAUL GOODMAN

The ending of Mr. Kadish's talk was curious, because he said at the beginning we don't have to have a *Weltbild* of what the university is and then he said in the end we have to inquire as to what the universities are about in order to answer most of the ticklish questions. Well, there it is. I'd like to run through his arguments in quick detail. He defines the rules as those things which are authoritatively defined—but obviously in interesting cases the question is always who *is* the authority, a legitimate authority. This is certainly the case in Berkeley, where one of the main complaints of the students was: Who are these Regents? I remember attending the first meeting of the Burns committee at Berkeley, and Savio got up and said, "Is it morally right for us to be talking to this man?" Burns was a charming man and it was obvious that all the students liked him, but was it morally right to be talking to him? After all, he was the appointee of the Regents and they were going to accept or decline, arbitrarily from the students' point of view, the report of the committee. You see, this was the committee on university reforms at Berkeley. Since he was not a free agent, but had to submit his report, unpublished, to the Regents, who could then say the devil with it (which in fact seems to be what they're doing), ought we to co-operate in any way with him? I think in interesting cases that is always the question. Now, when he says that the rules with sanctions obviously serve the interests of order—I quote him there—I don't think it's obvious at all that they always serve the interests of order. For instance, rules about moral conduct in the history of American legislation have almost always obviously resulted in disorder, like the prohibition law, or the narcotics law at present, which clearly is a chief cause of creating criminal behavior, as opposed to traffic rules, which do obviously serve the interest of order.

It happens that youth is a kind of feared minority in our society and the rules which obviously serve the interest of order generally, I think, increase repression and anxiety, and create criminality. Likewise, many sanctioned rules by authorities are founded, and I'm surprised that a jurist didn't bring this out, on spite and vengeance quite simply, and then it's a question as to whether one has to put up with the spite and vengeance of the rule makers, a very important reason and perhaps a good reason. I'm not ruling it out as a legitimate reason for the imposition of rules; you know, if the taboo is broken the gods will strike us all dead! And the women won't bear children, the cattle will die of the plague, etc. Therefore, it's necessary to take vengeance on the criminal. Now, I'm afraid a good many of our rules, especially applied to youth, are of that kind. Somehow the heavens are going to fall if these people are not kept in line. Then he says that the interests of freedom are often served by the imposition of rules; that is, they give a structure to society in which activity can operate. But since the imposition of the rules is not often so reasonable, and it cannot be in its principle because authority figures are power figures, this imposition might precisely have the opposite effect; it would be against the interests of freedom and in fact create disrespect for law. (Good traffic rules depend on respect for law.)

Jefferson, when he founded the University of Virginia, insisted on having the rules cut to a bare, bare-bones minimum because he said all these petty rules you make, about morals, etc., will surely create disrespect for law because young people will surely violate them. He said, therefore, every student has a front door and a back door to his dormitory room. Out the front door he puts on his tie and dresses well as befits a citizen of the University of Virginia. At the back door he can keep his horse and his whore. It's perfectly all right, he said, and there'll be no rules. In fact, the situation gets to be like Shay's Rebellion. You see, there is one reason for rules to produce order in the interests of freedom; it is to stop the kind of destruction which will prevent reconstruction of society, in which the problem can be solved more temperately. Well then, there's Shay's Rebellion in Jefferson's time, and Jefferson approved of the rebels' being stopped and disarmed, and then he said, "Now, let them go free, because if you don't let them go free we will discourage future rebellion." He said, "But it's very necessary that the people rebel continually." Otherwise, we can't have a democracy because obviously the laws are continually in process of change. Therefore, the correct method is to act as in an insane asylum; the trusty grabs the guy and maybe he has to put him in a strait jacket. But he's not going to punish him. You see, you can have enforcement of rules without sanction. That's a very important distinction to be made, and I don't think modern jurists like to make that distinction so much. That is, that you can have the common law without the cops except as insane-asylum trusties to maintain the king's peace, but once you've maintained the king's peace that doesn't mean you single the man out as a criminal. On the contrary, he's a rebel; now he's quiet; now life can go on. And at Berkeley the great mistake, obviously, that the administration made was to suspend the students; that was a mistake. Perfectly all right to stop the thing; but why did they suspend them? Because they had to pay off to outside forces.

Good rules should be of such a sort that due process is not violated; there should be proportionate punishment, etc. But what if, in fact, due process *is* violated as it was by Clark Kerr? Or if proportionality is violated, as for instance when the Congress of the United States assigned a *five-year* penalty for burning a piece of paper? You know, the great dignity of the draft boards is offended because somebody burned a piece of paper. Now, I trust the Supreme Court will strike that down, but it's not going to strike it down during the present crisis. Meanwhile, all these kids are being drafted. They can't wait five years to show their defiance of the draft law. It takes years to appeal! Now, in cases of police brutality, we set up a civilian review board. Well, the history of civilian review boards has been that three or four years later some little fraction of cases gets reviewed. The real issue is all over by then, and I submit that those are the interesting cases. You know, we aren't talking here abstractly, really.

Now, the question is: What should be left to the civil authorities and what is obviously the university's business? For instance, one of the things obviously the university's business is cheating on examinations. No! Suppose the students feel that the examination system itself as it is run is a hoax, or is a processing, a factory method? Which in fact it is! And smart students feel that—if examination is connected with grading, of course. If it's not connected with grading, examination is a fine teaching method. Many universities therefore put in an honor system saying the university will not have anything to do with organizing cheating, but the wise students, I think, object to the honor system because, they say, "You want us to police ourselves in departments where we don't think the law should exist in the first place; the institution shouldn't exist. And then you want us to police ourselves within that institution! In other words, we're supposed to be cops for a bad law which *we* have not made and which is to our disadvantage." See, it isn't really clear what is always obviously the university's business, and it's astonishing, historically, the way this matter has changed.

In the Middle Ages, the question of what should be left to the civil authorities and what should belong to the university was there for an entirely different reason. The question was not how the university should discipline the person for off-campus activities, but how the university should protect the person who obviously engaged in a civil crime! The Master of Arts got drunk and he raped the girl off campus. Ought the university go out and protect him? "Can we get away with it?"—that was the medieval question. That is, "He is one of ours." And here, I think, an extremely important thing comes up. Of course, the university is not a parent. I would agree with Mr. Kadish there. But the university *is* a community, and therefore it is not easy to make the simple division between what belongs to the university as a teaching academy and what belongs to it as a society having to do with citizens who are members of the community. If a university is going to operate, in some sense its people are special to itself.

This obviously happens with regard to the question of what is criticism. Ought the university to engage in activity of criticism? It's a question of what is university truth, after all. Now one of the things the students objected to and many professors object to is that university truth as it's gotten to be understood is "academic"; I mean by academic that it's not real. Then the question comes up of what is being taught in such a university where the truth is "academic" and is not supposed to have an effect in the world. And I submit to you that it's the academic attitude that's being taught, and that's exactly what the students object to. You see, you can't draw this distinction so easily, between the intellectual appraisal of things and the pragmatic working out of them in the world. Because often the only way to know whether you have the truth is to know if your proposition works out, and the only way to see if it works out is to try to make it work out! Well, are we then to teach sociology and discourage activism? It would be like trying to teach physics and forbidding laboratory work. No! If you're going to teach physics you're going to have to have laboratory work. If you're going to teach sociology you're going to have to take society, unfortunately, as your laboratory; it can't be helped. It's the nature of finding out!

Then, the question of what goes on on a campus. What is a campus? Do we mean the land? You see, a man's home is his castle, true; but a search warrant can invade that home. Well, now, what happens here is that the army, apparently, can invade the campus and recruit. Then I'm damned if I can see why the campus can't go outside and infest the recruiting stations! Really, I can't see the distinction in any logic, law, or morals. And frankly, in terms of good politics. What if, for instance, the general behavior of society is such that it undermines the very premises on which real professions exist? For instance, suppose there is in the community a crazy censorship of the press, or slanted news. Then it seems to me the duty of the humanists of that university to go out there in the society, if necessary organizing boycotts against a newspaper that censors; because it has to say that this kind of freedom of communication is necessary in society at large for the humanities to be taught in the university. It's obviously so. In other words, in order to defend the groundwork—the social groundwork—in which university work is possible, often the university has got to go out and fight in the outside society. This is not engaging in politics; politics is much too transient. But it *is* engaging in the defense of the foundations of Western civilization. It seems to me intolerable that any physics department, any university, would allow there to be classified scientific research. Not only on the campus, but in society as a whole. It must go out and protest. Not sabotage— but protest the existence of classified physics, because that's against the whole spirit of Western science which is precisely public and international. You know, that's the Galilean spirit. And yet our physics departments have supinely accepted even classified research on their own campuses, except for a few splendid cases like Chicago or Wisconsin. Probably on this very campus there's classified research being done.[1] That's an outrage! How can the faculty possibly accept that? Western civilization crumbles to the ground if that's accepted! You see, these are the interesting cases.

■ ## DISCUSSION

s. KADISH: About Mr. Goodman's comments on the general issue of rules and sanctions and order: He said first that it isn't so that rules obviously serve the interests of order—sometimes they do the contrary, they create disorder. I don't doubt that; foolish rules foolishly applied create disorder. I was talking only about the motive, the design; their purpose. Rules obviously are designed to encourage order.

The other point he made is that you can have rules without sanction. You can recognize a man as a rebel. Now he's quiet and you can say, "Okay, you can go on your way." Insofar as Mr. Goodman is suggesting a humane use of sanctions which will avoid imposing pain on individuals insofar as is consistent with the social purposes of rules and sanctions, I am with him altogether. I think, however, that it tends to make a travesty of the existence of rules if those in authority and with responsi-

[1] Case Institute of Technology has discontinued the conducting of classified research. A small amount is still conducted at Western Reserve.—Ed.

bility to enforce them characteristically and typically in all cases decline to fulfill the promise which the law holds out when it says, "Don't do this lest you be punished." There comes a point, therefore, when obviously some kinds of sanctions are called for.

The final point I want to make concerns Mr. Goodman's general approach to authority, which underlies all his observations. I would think Mr. Goodman is barking up the wrong tree! I think that the real hard question does not involve the extirpation of authority at all. The real hard, tough question of life is a political question. It's a hard-nosed problem of the kind that John Searle so vividly talked about. How do you domesticate authority? How do you make the existence of delegated authority tolerable and acceptable within the accepted tenets of a democratic community? These are the hard, real problems of life which I think would require the greatest amount of ingenuity and attention.

P. GOODMAN: I was thinking of things like the prohibition law and the narcotics law, which in fact aggravate a problematic moral situation by driving it into the hands of an underworld and therefore creating criminality and then new addicts, because "pushers" make money out of it. So it's possible that law, which can be moved for the most benevolent reasons, can in fact backfire and create the very things which it's supposed to attack. This is obviously true with delinquency law, etc. A large part of delinquency is created by the fact that delinquents are called delinquents—that young people are called delinquents. They then come on like delinquents, because if they're called delinquents and they're surveyed like delinquents, and they're treated like delinquents, they might as well *be* delinquents.

■

J. SEARLE: It's generally the case with freedom that if a completely irresponsible and unrestrained use of that freedom is made, then the social organization within which the freedom exists will break down. But it doesn't follow from that that the social organization should attempt to prevent that unrestrained and irresponsible use of the freedom by enacting regulations. This isn't just to do with the university—this is about society. Senator McCarthy, for example, had freedom of speech, and he also had certain freedoms of speech that are special to the floor of the Senate, and he never exceeded his freedom of speech. But we are all agreed both that if everybody behaves like that society would really be in a mess, and, at the same time, that his freedom of speech ought not to be restricted. This is a kind of paradox of democracy. But let me go through these examples. The so-called "obscenity crisis" was a major event. A university president resigned, and it was really extraordinary to hear grown men stand up in front of other grown men and say, "Never in my life have I been so *revolted*." Even in that crisis, though, nobody said there is a blanket university rule against obscene or forbidden words. That was never the point. The point was that it was a violation of the appropriate *manner* of exercising free speech to enforce obscenity on unwilling audiences. If you want to sell a pamphlet containing such words, and the pamphlet is within the law and the regulations of the University of California campus (that is, it's distributed by a registered student organization, and so on), you're entitled to do that. We have no blanket restrictions against forbidden words or ideas. The point was the *manner* in which they were invoked: on involuntary audiences. Now, similarly, with the other cases. If you accept certain kinds of democratic assumptions I think you have to accept that there are constraints available in a society other than simply regulatory constraints, and this is really the point I've been making. What we have are not sets of slogans but sets of objectives, and you try to reach those objectives in an *ad hoc* fashion, it's true, but one of the objectives is something like complete freedom of speech—no restriction on content.

w. METZGER: Generally I am on the side of those who would give students a great deal of room to speak. But I am not with those who would grant them blanket immunities from academic prosecution in matters relating to speech. A word may be the first evidence we have of the character of a psychopath: it would be irresponsible to insist that no action be taken to help or control him until his problem has taken other forms. Similarly, a word does not always communicate an opinion: it may commit an assault. The mouth is not necessarily a less violent organ than the fist. It would be irresponsible to insist that the authority of the university may not act against words that strike blows. Of course, we can't and probably shouldn't compile a lexicon of word-blows and use that as a basis for censorship; we must also beware of making the most delicate sensibilities the test of what is or is not wounding speech. But surely no one in this culture would be in any doubt that if I called a Jew a "kike" or if I called a Negro a "nigger," I would be assaulting him, not communicating with him, and that even if he were not very sensitive, he would have the right to regard me as his assailant. There would be less agreement on whether a four-letter word denoting intercourse, hurled at passers-by in a public place, is a similar form of aggression: I think it is, if malicious intent is involved. This touches on my misgivings about the Berkeley formula—"The content of speech shall not be restricted by the University": it seems to me to be much too unqualified. I know that it was passed in a hurry to rectify the errors of the past; but it seems to be committing another error, the error of sanctioning or seeming to sanction the notion that anything spoken goes.

V

BITS AND SNATCHES

V

◻ BITS AND SNATCHES

S. KADISH: It occurs to me to say that your observation raises a very important question, that of the limits of criticism within a university of the society which creates this university. But in my view you underestimate the vitality and flexibility of democratic institutions. It's remarkable what the public can be persuaded to tolerate through appeals to principles of freedom and through all kinds of rationalizations to comfort anxiety, like, "After all, professors are a bunch of kooks anyway, and they don't really matter." Actually, what on a priori grounds would seem to be totally unviable situations that couldn't be, actually are! And Berkeley is a living example. But there are others all over the country. We just happen to go into extremes in California. But Berkeley is a classic example of this paradox that a legislature, a community, *will* support a university, sometimes grudgingly, sometimes muttering and grumbling protestations. But it is prepared to accept it.

J. SEARLE: State-supported universities are dependent on state funds, and there are certain limits beyond which they won't go. But, all the same, we've been enjoying quite a bit of freedom at the University of California in Berkeley. You said that university administrations are really something like reflections of the power structure of the society. I don't think some members of the state legislature would like the idea that I'm their reflection, but I am a sort of administrator. So, my feeling about it is: We won't know if we don't try, and if we can't try in the universities then we just better give up altogether. Now what we're doing at Berkeley is trying!

■

S. KADISH: I think one of the many benefits of the student revolt was a more sensitized conscience on the part of the power structure to the importance of taking into account what the student had to say. This was perhaps immediately produced by a kind of fear, an apprehension of what will happen if you don't. But that sentiment after a while gives way to respect and appreciation of the value of what the student has to say, and I think that I see around me in Berkeley more and more semi-formalized ways of students' expressing judgment and preferences and gripes about various aspects of educational life. Just in the law school, for example, we have created a student-relations committee which consists of three members of the faculty and a number of student leaders. They meet regularly. Various suggestions are made by this group which are turned over to the faculty, and by and large so far the batting average is 100 per cent. (That's not going to continue. This is the honeymoon period.) But I think this kind of thing is happening all over and I wouldn't want my remarks to be interpreted as in any way suggesting that it's not a *wholly* desirable thing to look to the customer, to look to the student—to treat him with dignity as an individual of maturity and intelligence in making your decisions on what to teach, where to teach, how to do it, and so on. And I think more and more we are doing that.

■

P. GOODMAN: I think the question about ideals for a university is precisely a violation of ideals on freedom and order. Once you have an ideal, a utopian ideal, it's precisely a pre-planned position. What I would say we ought to do for our universities now, instead of just correcting them according to some prior notions, is to allow the professions to function as professions, the teaching of professions to function as teaching of professions. That's all I'm asking for! It's this big overall plan of the ideal of the university which I think is precisely wrong.

You know, M.I.T. is 80 per cent budgeted from the federal government and Columbia is 40 per cent budgeted; every student who goes into the university has had his time and way of life controlled by SAT, College Boards, curriculum approvements from the National Science Foundation, etc., so that he is processed into a kind of non-thinking creature by extramural pressures. Then, there is the degree-shaping attitude as well as the draft-dodging attitude—which is the chief reason for going to college now on the part of, let us say, 80 per cent of the students at any university in the country. I guess 80 per cent would not be there if they did not have to get a degree for economic reasons, or to avoid the draft. This certainly is something profoundly influencing university atmosphere. You know, this isn't a detail—this is the way, in effect; and I think if you blink at that you miss the facts about the present academic life.

■

J. SEARLE: The university is *not* a democracy. It should not be a democracy. It's an aristocracy. But you can have complete freedom in an aristocracy. I never really understood that until I lived in England. England's not a democracy, but it does have freedom, and what we're interested in in the university is not democracy, it's an aristocracy of intellect; some guys know more than others—they teach! But as far as freedom is concerned, you *can* grant freedom within this aristocratic system. Now, how do you make it work, given California politics? That's a tougher question.

■

P. GOODMAN: The reason we have democracy is that democracy is good for people because they learn something. One of the ways they learn, of course, is by making important mistakes and suffering the consequences. Offhand, either as a parent or when I used to be a therapist, I never found that there is such a thing as too much freedom. I have yet to observe the horrible consequences. There is such a thing as preventing a child from drinking poison medicine or running out into the street or falling out of a window, but beyond that my experience has been that an animal that hasn't been over-repressed is extremely prudent.

■

That the whole course of history has been one of developing extrinsic organizations is not true at all. If we take, say, the breakdown of the feudal system, the rise of the free towns, we had the development of new de-central free agencies. I think this was true with the breakdown of the mercantile system and the development of the free-enterprise system. I think this was true during especially the first part of the Reformation—the development of free churches against the previous hierarchical and repressive system. I think that the nationalist revolutions at the present time, the overthrow of imperialism, have been of that kind. In fact, I would go so far as to say that most of the valuable parts of Western culture have had their greatest development during the periods of breakdown of extrinsic organization and development of intrinsic organization. History books are extremely odd. When countries are great powers or at the top of their repressive organization, at that moment they loom large in history books, but if you go over to the other kind of books—the history of culture, or the history of social relations—then you don't find this true at all. You find that the countries which have dropped out of the history books, like Denmark, suddenly assume a great place because of their co-operative movement, etc. We now happen to be at a place in America where we are a great power; therefore, so long as we maintain that position, it is impossible that we should advance civilization, and the sooner we get the hell out of it, the better we'll be!

■

Let's talk about the handling of children—small children—in the last thirty years, as canonized, let's say, by Dr. Spock. With regard to masturbation, he says this is something all the little animals will do, good, smile at them and it's perfectly nice. If they tend to do only that all day it's very likely that something else is wrong, and look for what else is wrong but don't do anything about the masturbating all day! Hasn't our whole attitude with regard to the upbringing of children from zero to six become precisely in the direction that I've been asking for? Somehow, at age six this stops dead and we're back in the Middle Ages, except the Middle Ages were better!

■

W. METZGER: Universities in this country aren't fortresses: they weren't built to close their entrance-ways and stand siege. On the other hand, they are not just collections of properties, ready and willing to be taken over. In estimating their capacity for independence, I think it is wiser simply to regard them as organizations with specific maintenance needs. They cannot live on their own resources: this will usually incline them toward submissiveness. But they also must appear to be free places in order to recruit good men: this will sometimes push them into resistance. Sometimes these organizations bend to one social pressure and then another. Some years ago, the University of Illinois fired Professor Leo Koch for advocating premarital intercourse in a column of the student newspaper. It is pretty clear that the administration's primary concern was public relations, not sexual relations: a member of the University's Dad Association stirred up a storm about the teacher, and this was the year for the voting of appropriations. For its action, the University was censured by the A.A.U.P. and received a good deal of unfavorable publicity in the upper reaches of academe. A few years later, it faced a similar situation when Professor Revilo P. Oliver, a classics scholar who was a member of the Birch Society, declared in a published article that President Kennedy was an accomplice of the Communists, who assassinated him when he ceased to serve them well. Again, pressure mounted for dismissal. But the university, fearing to worsen its reputation in the academic marketplace, decided not to discipline the professor. The net result was that the institution lost an advocate of libido and retained an advocate of lunacy! But this can happen when an organization of this kind tries to maintain itself amid conflicting pressures.

■

P. GOODMAN: In a national economy the money is in federal funding. The question has to do with control of that money, and where decisions are made. The anarchist position is not a doctrinaire position of no government; that's not the point. It's a continual tendency to try to increase autonomy, autonomous units. For instance, the Bill of Rights is an anarchist document and was called so at the time it was proposed. Everybody said, like Mr. Kadish says, that the world will fall to pieces. It was said because how would you take care of such extreme cases, etc. This was all debated at that time. But the anarchists happened to be at the helm at that time and therefore pushed the doctrine through. Well, we don't mean by anarchism—anarchy; although they were called "anarchists"; that word was used. They meant: We're trying to increase the autonomy of individuals and of voluntary associations in the society. There isn't any reason why a great "funding" device couldn't be spontaneously adopted by all people who think about the question. How, in a national economy, do you tax Esso? You can't tax them on the corner because that's not where the money is; the money is down on Wall Street. Therefore, you have to tax the income of the corporation. Now, the only one who can tax the income of a national corporation is a national body.

VI

REFLECTIONS ON THE
NATURE OF THE PROBLEM:
Mortimer R. Kadish

VI

REFLECTIONS ON THE NATURE OF THE PROBLEM

Mortimer R. Kadish

A long and far-ranging discussion has played upon the question of that organization of the parts of the university, that relation of the university to its surrounding human environment, which would best preserve, along with the other interests of the university, the interests of "freedom" and/or "order," whatever these terms might ultimately mean. I shall not presume at this stage of the game to essay still another set of plans, prejudices, and aspirations for the proper ordering of universities—for this "ordering question" in which "order" is merely one value which might attach to a proper ordering. Instead, I shall pose another, thinner sort of question. What are we about when we ask the ordering question? What kind of thing counts as evidence for settling it? What notable ways of putting it obscure the question or beg it? What sort of solution or resolution ought one expect from that kind of question? Admitting that the preceding discussion has not entirely ignored even issues such as these, I propose to bring them front and center by (1) examining what at least seem to be some misformulations of the ordering question, (2) reformulating in a perhaps preferable way the nest of questions the ordering question in fact constitutes, and (3) testing for the possible limits of any proper expectation of a solution.

In consequence, the best and central portions of this book's contents—discussions of a freer and more varied education, of the concrete ways in which law provides for the values of both freedom and order, of *Lehrfreiheit* and *Lernfreiheit*, of the tangled problems of maintaining a university in its time of troubles—must pass without the consideration they deserve.

I. MISFORMULATIONS

1. To justify beginning a serious inquiry into the problem of properly ordering universities, still another objection must first be registered against construing that problem as a choice between a "natural" or "spontaneous" ordering on one hand and an "imposed" and "artificial" ordering on the other. For if this is the choice, there is no problem unless it be the technological one of eliminating the established order. Obviously, the "natural" is better than the "imposed," if these be the alternatives; and no member of the symposium, it seems safe to say, would deny it.

Yet I think there is a complex and difficult problem even for educational institutions, where it seems relatively easy to prescribe the effacing of administration and all other forms of "external" constraint upon student and faculty. Therefore, I must suggest why the terms of the choice won't do and why putting the ordering question as though they would represents a significant misformulation.

First, then, even assuming some set of purposes or functions in some non-trivial sense "natural" to man, the question remains: *How* shall human nature achieve its natural grace and freedom, in what guise, through what means? Let it be the case that agreement on what grace and freedom are would follow immediately upon the removal of imposed prejudices—and this is an inordinately large assumption—still, between the potentiality and the achievement intervene a technology and a specific history, hence a choice. Perhaps recourse to free functioning and natural grace will enable us to say, as Mr. Goodman so often and perceptively does, that here and here stands an abomination that custom and interest disguise. But surely such perceptions, as the frequent agreement between Mr. Goodman and the other symposiasts who do not share his metaphysics suggests, may be justified on other grounds; his standards, facing toward the ultimate good, leave us terribly adrift, prophets without proposals in a world in which the dismantling of even an "imposed" order can hardly be depended upon to result in a better, wiser ordering. The "natural," alas, is not all that natural. Such is the moral of more than one revolution.

Consider, besides, the other side of the choice Mr. Goodman sets us: an "imposed" order. An order might indeed be imposed upon people from "outside," which is his picture of the alternative to the freedom of anarchy. Yet this side of anarchy there are many stops, and many roads branching off to a variety of destinations other than sheer tyranny. This is, I take it, the justification of the effort to achieve a democratic politics and, as well, the point of Mr. Kadish's entire discussion of the freedom-making use of law. The preference for a "functional order" over a non-functional one, which all the symposiasts must share, does not necessarily forbid any effort to discriminate and choose proper and rational sanctions over brutal and unjust penalties, or to consider carefully when and where to impose any sanctions at all. Nor does that preference as such forbid marking out in advance the rules for building our societies, if those rules are based upon the best available evidence. The anarchist's answer represents only one kind of answer to the ordering question engendered by the conditions of social life and cannot establish its right by principles which beg the question—as, I take it, making our choice a choice between nature and imposition does.

Yet let the Goodman choice be the choice: even so, some repressive orders might be imposed by methods still less manageable and more destructive than the methods of the police, "spontaneously," as the crying need for civil rights legislation has testified. Against the informal pressures of exclusion, contempt, and discrimination, the anarchic society may have still less means of protecting itself than our own.

2. There is, however, a more prevalent and riskier way of misformulating the ordering question than Mr. Goodman's ingenious combination of anarchy and Aristotle. Instead of "natures," ascribe "purposes" or "functions" to institutions. As Mr. Searle puts it, "The purpose of the university is the advancement and dissemination of knowledge . . . in less euphemistic terminology, 'teaching and research.'" Given those purposes, he offers two

possible definitions of academic freedom, two (partial) ways of ordering the university: the "minimal" or "A.A.U.P." definition of academic freedom, according to which "academic freedom is derived from and is restricted to the special needs of the academy" and the "maximal" or "FSM" definition, according to which "anything goes as long as it's legal and it does not interfere with the normal functions of the university"—which are, of course, teaching and research, along with certain "subsidiary" affairs. There is much more, of course. My point is that Mr. Searle's "purposes" or "functions" will not provide an adequate basis for ordering the university according to either the A.A.U.P. or the FSM definitions, and that their use misrepresents the practical choice.

The clue is that Mr. Searle, despite having made the attempt, cannot escape the notion that the primary functions of the university *are* teaching and research and that he can't convince the students he would like to convince. As he puts it, "They reject the assumption that the purposes of a university are education and research and favor the view that the main purpose of the university is to effect social change." Mr. Searle is an extremely convincing man—he shares a great many of his students' perspectives. Why can't he convince them? Why does *he* remain convinced— and uncomfortable in the conviction?

There are many reasons, no doubt, but I should like to concentrate on the reasons germane to the formulation problem. Teaching, research, and effecting social change are not, as he (and Mr. Kadish also) seems to assume, rival purposes on an equal footing. His students are right. Teaching and research are not the ends of the university any more than turning wheels is the purpose of the automobile. At the same time, of course, the university proceeds through teaching and research just as the automobile does by turning its wheels. His students see that teaching and research may achieve a variety of purposes. Mr. Searle sees what his students have been led to deny by placing on the same bench, just as he does, teaching, research, and social change: that teaching and research are the characteristic *means* through which the university functions. Hence his "agonizing" reappraisals never persuade him to drop teaching and research, or to minimize them, despite his own high valuation of social change of the sort many of his students have in mind. An institution in which the main mechanisms of action were *not* teaching and research would not be called a "university." It is no wonder that an argument so misconstrued cannot be resolved.

It might, of course, be answered that the students who denied teaching and research as purposes of the university really wanted to dismantle the university—as someone who wanted to deny turning wheels to be the purpose of the automobile might really want to dismantle the automobile. Then there would be a real enough clash of views, but the clash would not be about the purposes of the university any more than it would be about the purposes of automobiles. If the purposes of the university indeed concern his students—as, for example, they concern Mr. Goodman, who, though he may speak of eliminating administration and various complexities, has, so far as I know, no word against teaching or research as such—then the argument between Mr. Searle and his students has not yet included a difference over that concern.

But does not a difference of value and attitude still remain between Mr. Searle and those of his students who insist on the priority of "changing society" over "teaching and research"? Obviously, Mr. Searle wants to do more of one thing at the university, his activist students another. But the point is only that the terms of their conflict are wrong; and now I would like to add that to put it his way to those whose values and attitudes differ in priorities from his own constitutes a dodge and an unwitting deception. For perhaps when Mr. Searle and his colleagues say "teaching and research" they presuppose in fact, though not in form, some accustomed content and some accustomed procedure or method—which is why a student activist might well bridle at teaching and research as proper ends. Professors tend to employ the obviousness of teaching and research as characteristic means to cast a spurious self-evidence upon teaching and research policies requiring for their justification the specific acceptance of ends which are just the ones at issue, of priorities just the priorities at stake:

(a) Does the promotion of social change come within the

purview of the university? To be sure, "effecting social change" is not "teaching." But may not teaching effect social change? Effecting social change may even be taught directly, as effectively or ineffectively as many other things. There is no logical or, so far as I can see, pedagogic objection against a course in Intermediate Revolution. Not the teaching "function" prohibits it, only the notion, right or wrong, that such a course ought not to be given; and to support this conclusion requires all manner of unstated presumptions about what universities are for.

(b) Anyway, it might be said, whatever the case with introductory courses, Intermediate and Advanced Revolution need practical work in society—which removes the business of teaching them from the university. But laboratory courses exist in many subjects. Medical students at Western Reserve University learn medicine partly by working in the community. The difference must be that teaching revolutionary tactics seems a mistake in principle for the university because we are unaccustomed to including revolution in the teaching process. Yet an effective choice has nevertheless been made.

(c) Like considerations obtain for the content of research. It is not self-evident that the only legitimate subject matters for university research are those standard for the major institutions. The content and direction of research refuse to stay fixed anyway. There can be no right to justify presently accustomed investigations against new contestants by the nature of "research" itself, though there is a temptation.

(d) Similarly, while I share the view that the methods of research must always in some sense exhibit the methods of intelligence rather than prejudice and blind morality, many modes of investigation which might lodge a claim to such a general commitment seem to many to fall outside the "proper" limits of university inquiry—particularly when they concern questions of ethics, sexual morality, or use of drugs. Also, people have been known to differ over what constitutes intelligent behavior or even "scientific method." Unstated notions of propriety which have little to do with research methods as such often determine the nature of "research."

Accordingly, the confusion of ends and the characterizing means of academic institutions obscures the decisions to be made and fails to resolve disagreement over the ordering of universities at just those points where the ordering is in serious question and purposes are at issue. Not that professors in general, let alone Mr. Searle, are blind to the concrete issues involved in the content and method of their teaching and research. Emphatically, however: They do not help themselves, or their students, by formulating the ordering problem in terms which disguise those issues.

3. Mr. Kadish urges that "the essential task in defining conduct which is appropriate for rule making and distinguishing it from conduct that is not is to determine the existence of a legitimate regulatory interest or concern by the university." Now I propose that the problem of ordering the university, even in the restricted respects which here concern Mr. Kadish, is misleadingly put as the problem of identifying "legitimate regulatory concerns." The legally transposed versions of Mr. Searle's purposes, such "concerns" are only verbally "essential."

The question of university regulation of "assaultive obscenity" illustrates Mr. Kadish's difficulty. If indeed the "essential task" in deciding whether the university may control assaultive obscenity is "to determine the existence of a legitimate regulatory interest or concern," then the determination of the existence of such a concern must lead *in a non-trivial way* to the conclusion, "Regulate (or do not regulate) assaultive obscenity." The method of determining the existence of a concern now becomes crucial. It must be done in such a way that that concern becomes indispensable to the argument. Yet, as a matter of fact, the good reasons Mr. Kadish offers for regulating assaultive obscenity—to protect the "wires of communication," etc.—while good reasons indeed, are good reasons for the *conclusion*, not for the *existence* of a legitimate regulatory interest. If, that is, they lead to the conclusion that the university has a legitimate regulatory concern with assaultive obscenity, they lead with equal directness to the ultimate conclusion that the university ought to control assaultive obscenity, *without* requiring as a premise to the argument what has already been established: that the university has here a legitimate regulatory concern. It turns out that if you can say that the university ought to do such and such, then the university has a legitimate regulatory concern in doing so; and that if you say the university has a legitimate regulatory concern, that only means the university ought to do so and so. Hence the criterion of a legitimate regulatory concern is not essential in defining conduct at all, but a way of solemnizing conclusions reached on other grounds.

Of course, Mr. Kadish himself limits the force and value he attributes to his legitimate regulatory concerns, and acknowledges that debate about such concerns requires agreement on the ends or functions of the university. Without rehashing the "function and purpose" discussion, it is well to recall that the parties to the campus debate, which the existence of legitimate regulatory concerns must help resolve, disagree precisely over what the university and its activities are for. Hence it remains mysterious how Mr. Kadish can consider a legitimate regulatory concern as even a weak tool. Perhaps he does so because agencies exist which do indeed assert regulative interests and assert them meaningfully. The assertion, of course, occurs within the framework of a body of law, where a system of courts exists to make agency decisions binding. If, therefore, universities can successfully assume legitimate regulatory concerns, their actions acquire more substantial justification than at first appears plausible, and determining the existence of a legitimate regulatory concern will constitute a genuine, if partial, solution of the ordering question. Unfortunately, however, no requisite body of law for universities exists which is also not at issue. Appeals to legitimate regulatory concerns, therefore, reduce to the hope that eventually there may be such a body of law applied by the courts to *grant* the university a legitimate regulatory concern in proscribing assaultive obscenity.

4. The last point in this brief lexicon of instructive ways not to deal with the problem of a proper ordering is primarily cautionary, since I am not sure just what kind of force Mr. Metzger intends for his discussion of the history of academic freedom, *Lehrfreiheit*, and *Lernfreiheit*. Not that I doubt the truth or interest of the discussion—only its evidential weight in the problem of a proper ordering. For attempts to provide "real definitions" of academic freedom, which indeed involve history, are logically independent of the question of what agency, if any, *ought* to control the parts of

the university, whether certain exemptions ought to extend to students, and so on. The wider definition of academic freedom Mr. Metzger seems finally to prefer may be preferable to Mr. Hook's. All the same, it remains open for anyone who concludes that one sort of ordering is more appropriate than another which more closely corresponds to common usage of "academic freedom," simply to give up, with logical equanimity, and without in any way weakening his position or any of the arguments favoring it, his appeal to academic freedom. He has surrendered a persuasion, not an argument: and that this is all becomes the more manifest if, as ought to be old hat, the "rights" of students or faculty are not objects to be discovered but constructions to be instituted, proposals for the conduct of affairs to be made good.

Accordingly, formulations of the ordering problem in terms of the "nature" of academic freedom cannot help very much, although appeals to academic freedom may nevertheless constitute powerful persuasions. On reflection, perhaps something similar might be said also of the other formulations of the problem: They are, in substantial measure, regardless of the honorable intentions of their proponents, propaganda, not serious efforts to manage a difficulty.

II. FORMULATIONS

Considering the proper ordering of universities raises a complex question of the sort central to any grasp of the theory of social action. The task now is, with the help of what has gone before, to construct that question and to suggest its significance for the present controversy. The ordering question, accordingly, can best be formulated in terms of three essentially connected positions:

1. *The problem of ordering the university exists as a problem in politics—a political problem.* Whatever the details of the recent events at Berkeley and on other campuses in the nation, one moral, I think, comes pre-eminently to the fore: students, faculty, administration, and community at large each have specific interests; these interests, while they may often overlap or reinforce one another, are not, despite the rhetoric of the "University" and its noble functions, identical or necessarily compatible. This is, I take

it, the point which in different ways concerns Messrs. Metzger, Kadish, and Searle. Contrary to the official terms of discussion, the university is a political institution; accordingly, consideration must be given to the various interests of the groups which make up the institution, and *including the interest of each group to announce and defend its own interests as it sees them.*

This last is of the essence. Even non-political institutions, like jails, may recognize positive clashes of interest but, by suppressing any announcement and defense of those interests, systematically and deliberately suppress politics. Since the rhetoric of the "University" and its unexceptionable purposes has tended to exempt universities, like other philanthropic institutions, from responsibility for what they do to people, and to justify strange tyrannies, the political description will take belaboring. Even at the "University" no major interest group, no matter how benign, adequately represents the substantive interests of another such group; and, clearly, no other group can in any degree represent that most fundamental of political interests, to announce and defend one's own interest as one sees it. As faculty scoffs at administration assurances of having the best interests of faculty at heart, so might—so does—a wide-awake student body deride an analogous claim in their behalf of a faculty bent upon making careers in their own profession and molding education to their own professional ends. And even Mr. Goodman's 99-per-cent administration-free collections of teachers and scholars, given the scarcities of time, brains, and resources, might soon experience and acknowledge the strains of differences not satisfactorily managed by parting company. Similarly for the community at large and the administrative class, which receive short shrift indeed from the symposiasts: even their interests do not readily dissolve in other peoples'.

How, then, meet the disparity and clash of interests? How, if the conflict is real, resolve it? In the normal way, by politics. The problem of the university poses a political problem in the sense both that the persons in the university are involved in politics (Mr. Searle's focus), and that they must establish a framework of rules for the conduct of that politics, must set up a binding and controlling structure (Mr. Kadish's).

The two most popular ways of denying—and, hence, underlining—the importance of the political problem these days are: first, the Platonic dodge, usually performed by faculty, according to which the true governance of the university rests upon the authority of those who know; and, secondly, the moralistic dodge, according to which no claim can be or ought to be considered, on pain of a sell-out, except the claim of the simple, righteous heart.[1] In both instances, the political order of the university is systematically denied. There are also other ways of dodging the political problem, such as the substitution of managerial models for political models by administrations and boards of trustees, or of complementary consumer models by students who do not see why they cannot have what they want when they are paying for it.

2. That the problem of ordering the university is not only a problem of politics but a problem of ends and of vision emerges with at least equal clarity from the symposiasts' discussion. In his unremitting stress upon that point lies, I think, Mr. Goodman's primary contribution. *The problem of the proper ordering of the university exists as a cognitive problem,* a problem of *knowing* the good, deciding on the true and the right, or at least the probable and the preferable, in the interests of which people operate within the political rules and seek to change them. What is a university for? The prevarications spoken of in Part I set aside, the laborious, detailed task remains of formulating that context of social and human action within which the university will receive a function. The task of ordering the university cannot be solely a political problem; and I take it that the discomfort with the "multiversity," which all the symposiasts express or imply, develops just because the multiversity loses the choice of ends and of vision in a political mediation among political interests—whatever those interests may be found to be and according to such strength as they may be found to have.

The point has been used by others: In the name of "teaching and research," the university promotes a society where individual

---

[1] I would therefore suggest that the objection of Mr. Searle's student activists to "compromise, conciliation, negotiation, and discussion," combined with their commitment to direct action, constitutes not, as he says, a "style" of politics, but the systematic *denial* of politics. To make a "stylistic" issue of the quarrel with the "liberal establishment" blurs the nature and the importance of the conflict.

freedom diminishes into a chance to succeed in the rat race. Higher education systematically, if covertly, trains "individuals" for the economic-technological machine or "establishment." Therefore, dissolve the university. Whether one agrees or not, a relevant reason has been advanced for a resolution of the ordering problem. Similarly, Mr. Goodman's objection that Mr. Kadish seeks to escape, but in the end cannot, the need for a *Weltbild* in setting up the university's rules and regulations, is a well-taken point regardless of how well taken it may be against this opponent in particular. To be sure, introducing the *Weltbild* into a discussion which might otherwise obtain working agreements is to be postponed until the last possible moment. But its interjection prior to that moment is a *political* mistake, not a logical one. The *logical* mistake is systematically to deny the cognitive question, the question of ends and vision, when handling *de facto* clashes of interest—for example, the very pertinent question whether or not some interest group expressing itself in the political arena *ought* not (in virtue of the kind of *Weltbild* determined upon for managing that arena) be excluded from consideration.

Concretely: While I am not sure whether or to what extent Mr. Searle would, if he could, minimize the influence of the Board of Regents and the community at large upon the Berkeley campus, he seems easily to accept the active presence in campus organizations of persons who have no particular relationship to the university as such and who, he says, use students and student organizations for their own purposes. Why does the mere presence and influence of this latter group give them a voice? Here is no longer a problem of the political organization of the university, but a "cognitive" problem gone unconsidered in the effort to handle revolt on the campus, with the effect that those are included whom Mr. Searle wishes to include and those excluded whom Mr. Searle wishes to exclude.

Or consider a second case of the demand of the cognitive problem to press beyond the institutional framework to the network of ends and interests constituting society at large—a demand which goes for all practical purposes ignored. Let us grant that academic freedom in some sense applies to students, that it implies freedom of advocacy, and that this freedom of advocacy, if real, implies *some* organizational machinery which the university ought to provide. It still is unclear why universities ought to provide "forums" for students and (I am tempted to call them) metics, thus making possible for them social and political action *beyond* the conceivable reach of the majority of citizens outside the university. Criticizing Mr. Metzger, Mr. Searle wonders what free speech means "if you don't own a newspaper or radio station"— and he makes it clear that students ought to have free speech in a meaningful sense of the phrase. But how *could* a nation of close to 200,000,000 distribute in a remotely equal way the instruments of free speech? There seems to be no objection raised to the unequal distribution among citizens and legislators of voting rights on bills. But I don't wish to belabor the obviously general considerations which go into justifying the extension of exceptional political privileges to students. The force of raising the issue at all is merely to illustrate the way in which a certain kind of conceptual scheme—in this case the scheme associated with the notion of academic freedom—can in practical discussion insulate proposals from the need to press the cognitive questions.

3. For the problem of a proper ordering of universities, however, it does not suffice even to acknowledge a political and a cognitive problem. The ordering problem exists in a more subtle and fundamental way still, as a decision problem in rational social action engendered by the simultaneous presence of a political and a cognitive problem in complex interdependence. The attempt to deal with the university must establish a specific kind of relation between what once would have been called the "real" and the "ideal," or, more recently, "means" and "ends-in-view." *The ordering problem is a problem in rationality*; and, therefore, it is the problem at fever pitch. Without faulting the symposiasts for not specifically having raised it in this form—a form I know to be quite familiar to some of them—I believe that the task assumed here of articulating the nature of the ordering problem demands that the requirements of the rationality question receive due notice.

Determining a proper ordering for universities, then, consists in choosing from among a range of alternatives a policy or program which will maximize pay-offs (the values explored in the cognitive problem); minimize the risk or probability of failure for selected pay-offs; and minimize, as well, the investment or sacrifice required to bring the end about (the political problem). Such, roughly, is the decision problem for any rational social action, and the point is to see how it applies.

Take, for an example of a program, what I believe to be Mr. Goodman's—the proposal to eliminate administration over and above janitorial and other service functions and to substitute small, more or less free associations of teachers and scholars. The reader may supply any values he likes for the ends, risks, and investments of those proposals. The following sort of schedule of tasks will constitute the decision problem for the Goodman program, or any other, and delineate in some of its complexity the nature of the evidence relevant to a solution.

(a) At some point in the game, a decision for or against the program will require coming to grips with certain peculiar features of the program as such. This will mean establishing an ordering of pay-offs on some preference scale in order to decide how much one wants the program in relaton to anticipations of what that program is likely to produce. It will also mean determining alternative courses of action ("instrumentalities") for instituting the program, and it will mean estimating the probabilities of those instrumentalities' doing the job and the cost of those instrumentalities. Lastly, since there are usually different probabilities for different instrumentalities' achieving specific programs, and since those instrumentalities themselves exact varying costs, it is necessary to face the delicate task of charging off the probability of success against a greater or less degree of probability.

An "unrealistic" program will achieve an acceptable probability of success for some given end at too great a cost. The Goodman program may conceivably be called unrealistic in this sense. On the other hand, there may exist more than one "realistic" choice of instrumentalities.

(b) Sooner or later the time comes in rational action for facing alternative programs as alternatives. That was the final justification of the symposium as a whole. Alternative programs must be set against each other, and each must receive the kind of analysis indicated in (a). "Rationality" requires lining up competing programs for the transformation, or the securing, of the status quo.

Those programs lined up, the climactic task set by the quest for rational choice is to choose among the available realistic programs, where no program exists such that its pay-off is the greatest, the investment or sacrifice required the least, and the probability of success the highest. Where such a program does exist, the matter is, of course, conclusively settled. However, the programs proposed in actual controversies to handle difficult cases rarely if ever possess such clear superiority. Such facts as that most of us are willing to pay more for one thing than another or to bet larger sums for smaller chances of success for some ends than for larger probabilities for others, continually disturb the calculation. Hence rational action will not consist in adopting the policy of the "idealist" who systematically chooses the program aimed to produce simply the best or noblest end, as though cost or probability were no consideration; nor, equally, will it consist in the "practical" man's choice of the cheapest or the most probable course of action. On the contrary, it will consist in the choice of an optimal combination of pay-offs, costs, and probabilities.

(c) To handle the Goodman program, therefore, or any other, will require establishing preference scales superordinate to the preference scales along which each proponent of a program orders his choices. Finally, for any deep controversy—and the controversy over the proper ordering of a university I take to be such a controversy—this procedure entails an indefinitely extensive plumbing of a network of preferences. That plumbing will demand, first, more factual knowledge of consequences and probabilities than is usually available; secondly, an indefinite articulation of social ends; and thirdly, a grasp of interrelationships among those ends and their conditions and consequences which did not, in all probability, begin to be grasped at the beginning. Termination comes when the parties to the controversy agree on the superordinate preference scale.

In partial consequence of the cognitive and political problem, then, securing a proper ordering poses some such decision problem and some such set of considerations. I do not pretend, in elucidating even as inadequately as above the problem's complexity and the net of considerations any answer entails, to have presented a routine for solving the problem, or to have done more than common sense, gently pressed, would do itself. I could not provide a complete statement of the logic and mathematics of decision theory for social action in so short a space even if I knew how, which, of course, I do not.

Nevertheless, be it observed, even if the degree of formalization achieved by decision theory in economics will never prove possible for such problems as ordering universities, and even on the rejection of the conceivable relevance of numerical techniques and utility scales to such problems, still the considerations this small survey presents are actually implicit in the course of argument the symposiasts have presented—implicit, crucial, and only intermittently come to specific issue. Hence I would urge, even if the parties to the discussions had reached agreement, that that agreement would be accidental, and not the product at all of the logic of their problem.[2]

III. LIMITS

Assuming now that a course of social action has been rationally decided upon and put into effect—and the difficulty is great enough to make comprehensible the kinds of simplifications and misformulations described—there exist fundamental limits on what ought to be expected of the solution. Some consciousness of those limits might serve at once to make argument more sober and to reduce that disillusionment with reasoning which usually follows wrong expectations.

Suppose, then, that a program has been settled upon for handling the ordering problem, in response to the political, cognitive,

[2] The "logic of the problem," it may be worth noting, also clarifies some classical theories of rational action. So Marx and Hegel, concerned with the relations of historical reality and objective value as the key to a rational social action, in effect assert that there exists only one "realistic" program for society which produces desirable ends. At least, that is a partial translation of their views. And Dewey, to the degree that he regards the decision problem in society as art-like, subject to the same kind of consideration encountered in painting or sculpture, sees ends and instrumentalities but neglects costs— which, perhaps, may be a way of stating his view that in truly rational behavior means are absorbed into ends and there is no sacrifice in the right decision, no means "merely" means.

and rationality questions. The point is that solutions are always and inevitably incomplete and provisional. They are incomplete in that they do not remove all difficulties; they are provisional in the obvious sense that even with respect to those of the problem's conditions which have been understood and met, mistakes might be made and, further, *better* solutions eventually devised. "Rationally," no program is final. But provisionality does not concern me here: it has been harped upon enough. Incompleteness, on the other hand, does, since the failure to come to terms with it seems at present a far more likely source of confusion. Also, logically, it is more interesting. Where provisionality marks the sense in which a rational believer holds his beliefs—provisionally—incompleteness marks the beliefs themselves and affects their justification.

Practically speaking, then, incompleteness means that it is wrong to expect of any program put forth to resolve the problems generated at any time within a society by some specific institution, such as the university of the present argument, that it justify itself by answering all possible objections. If in response to a program someone asks, "But what about such and such?" or "What if you do this and that happens?" one ought to expect times when the only proper answer is, "We'll have to see what happens," or "We'll have to *hope* that such and such does not take place," or even, "Well, what would *you* suggest?" All this is practical wisdom. The point is that it *is* wisdom, not just making do.

All institutions are in varying degree fragile, the fragility intrinsic to the fact that each is but one institution within a changing society. From the contingency of institutions follows the incompleteness of justifications; if a justification could be complete for any program, all difficulties could be solved and the institution would have ceased to be fragile.

Reviewing the complex problem involved in a proper ordering of universities makes the point more particular:

1. If the ordering problem is seen as a political problem, nothing is more traditional than the incompleteness of the programs offered for resolving those problems. Assuming that a prime condition of political orders is the recognition of the interest to defend an interest as one sees it, then the radical instability of political solutions of political problems becomes transparent. For

no interest group will ever see the substantive interest of another group the way that other group sees it, or place the same weight upon either the substantive interest of that other group or upon its interest in defending that substantive interest.

2. If the ordering problem is also a cognitive problem (in the present sense of a problem of ends and of vision), the fragility of universities and the incompleteness of programs becomes still more apparent. It is not merely that history pulls the justification for any institution, as well as the conditions for its sheer existence, out from under that institution, although, of course, that is part of it. There is, obviously, no final justification. But still more: There is no *complete* justification because a complete justification for the ends produced by any specific program would presuppose a society organized like chess, in which there is one great end, checkmate. For playing the game of proper orderings in society, there is never checkmate—at most, given the nature of the rule set, check.

3. If the ordering problem is a problem of rational action, and any competent judge of orders must balance off the weights or values he attributes to the programs he must judge—and, indeed, assign those weights or values in the first place—then the final arbitrariness and contingency of practical judgments becomes manifest not as an affair ten miles away (present, but not practically relevant), but relevant like the sand beneath one's feet. One feels the ground give every moment one "calculates" one's judgment; and it remains a puzzle why one must automatically accept one's own balance sheets of yesterday any more than the balance sheet of someone else.

In conclusion, then: Universities, as perhaps the oppositions and the puzzlements of the symposiasts have illustrated, are open, both in their existence and in their justification, to perpetual question. Only a theory closed to the demands of rationality separates the two kinds of open-ness—which, of course, is the Hegelian point in slightly different language. We can only hope, therefore, that the conditions of society will continue to sustain the universities in a useful growth: that people will not turn into haters of knowledge; that the values of compromise, discussion, and the like, which Mr. Searle finds his students questioning and which I think are fairly considered the "political" values, will not weaken too much in the population; that the larger community will not become excessively frightened of injury to its own interest—against which danger it possesses, as much as the groups within the university, a legitimate right to defend itself. The list could be lengthened. Yet none of the elements in that list would be more than partially (I am tempted to say, for the peculiarly delicate affair which is the university, peripherally) within the control of university action.

It is only necessary to remember that while the existence and justification of universities remain open to question, the specific, delicate task of ordering the university which Mr. Kadish articulates, and the business of running it which Mr. Searle presents, are not therefore rendered impossible, but all the more necessary, as perpetual challenges.

Appendix I

STATEMENT ON THE ACADEMIC FREEDOM
OF STUDENTS*

Upon the recommendation of Committee A on Academic Freedom
and Tenure in October, 1960, the Council authorized appointment of
a new standing committee, designated as Committee S on Faculty
Responsibility for the Academic Freedom of Students. Dr. Phillip
Monypenny, Professor of Political Science at the University of Illinois,
was appointed to serve as Chairman of the new committee. Once
established, Committee S gave primary attention to the task of formulating a statement on the academic freedom of students. Several drafts
were prepared, one of which was published with the consent of the
Council in the Autumn, 1964, issue of the AAUP Bulletin for the express purpose of inviting reaction and comments from members, chap-
ters, conferences, and other interested persons and organizations.

The preliminary Committee S statement stimulated considerable interest and response. Committee S therefore directed most of its attention during 1965 to refining the tentative statement published in
1964. The statement which follows has been approved by the Council
in principle but remains a tentative, rather than a fixed, statement of
Association policy. The Council has also authorized Committee S to
initiate discussions with representatives of other interested national
organizations in the hope that these efforts might result in the formulation of a joint statement on student rights and responsibilities. These
discussions will commence this winter.

The Members of Committee S who prepared the following statement
are:
Phillip Monypenny (Political Science) University of Illinois (Chairman)

* Reprinted from the A.A.U.P. Bulletin, Winter, 1965.

Philip Appleman (English) Indiana University
Frederick H. Hartmann (Political Science) University of Florida
Beatrice G. Koneheim (Physiology) Hunter College
John J. Reed (History) Muhlenberg College
Tom J. Truss, Jr. (English) University of Mississippi
William Van Alstyne (Law) Duke University
Robert Van Waes (History) Washington Office

PREAMBLE

Free inquiry and free expression are essential attributes of the community of scholars. As members of that community, students should be encouraged to develop the capacity for critical judgment and to engage in a sustained and independent search for truth. The freedom to learn depends upon appropriate opportunities and conditions in the classroom, on the campus, and in the larger community. The responsibility to secure and to respect general conditions conducive to the freedom to learn is shared by all members of the academic community. Students should endeavor to exercise their freedom with maturity and responsibility.

I. In the classroom

The professor in the classroom and in conference should encourage free discussion, inquiry, and expression. Students should be evaluated solely on the basis of their academic performance, not on their opinions or conduct in matters unrelated to academic standards.

A. *Protection of Freedom of Expression.* Students are responsible for learning thoroughly the content of any course of study, but they should be free to take reasoned exception to the data or views offered, and to reserve judgment about matters of opinion.

B. *Protection Against Improper Academic Evaluation.* Students are responsible for maintaining standards of academic performance established by their professors, but they should have protection through orderly procedures against prejudiced or capricious academic evaluation.

C. *Protection Against Improper Disclosure.* Information about student views, beliefs, and political associations which professors acquire in the course of their work as instructors, advisers, and counselors should be considered confidential. Protection against improper disclosure is a serious professional obligation. Judgments of ability and character may be provided under appropriate circumstances.

II. Student Records

Institutions should have a carefully considered policy as to the information which should be part of a student's permanent educational record and as to the conditions of its disclosure. To minimize the risk of improper disclosure, academic and disciplinary records should be separate, and the conditions of access to each should be set forth in an explicit policy statement. Transcripts of academic records should contain only information about academic status. Data from disciplinary and counseling files should not be available to unauthorized persons on campus or to any person off campus except for the most compelling reasons. No records should be kept which reflect the political activities or beliefs of students. Provision should also be made for periodic routine destruction of non-current disciplinary records. Administrative staff and student personnel officers should respect confidential information about students which they acquire in the course of their work.

III. Student Affairs

In student affairs, certain standards must be maintained if the academic freedom of students is to be preserved.

A. *Freedom from Arbitrary Discrimination.* Colleges and universities should be open to all students who are academically qualified. While sectarian institutions may give admission preference to students of their own persuasion, such a preference should be clearly and publicly stated. College facilities and services should be open to all students, and institutions should use their influence to secure equal access for all students to public facilities in the local community.

B. *Freedom of Association.* Students bring to the campus a variety of interests previously acquired and develop many new interests as members of the academic community. They should be free to organize and join associations to promote their common interests.

1. Affiliation with an extramural organization should not of itself affect recognition of a student organization.

2. Each organization should be free to choose its own campus adviser, and institutional recognition should not be withheld or withdrawn solely because of the inability of a student organization to secure an adviser. Members of the faculty serve the college community when they accept the responsibility to advise and consult with student organizations; they should not have the authority to control the policy of such organizations.

3. Student organizations may be required to submit a current list

of officers, but they should not be required to submit a membership list as a condition of institutional recognition.

4. Campus organizations should be open to all students without respect to race, religion, creed, or national origin, except for religious qualifications which may be required by sectarian organizations.

5. Students and student organizations should be free to examine and to discuss all questions of interest to them, and to express opinions publicly or privately. They should also be free to support causes by any orderly means which do not disrupt the regular and essential operation of the institution.

6. Students should be allowed to invite and to hear any person of their own choosing. While the orderly scheduling of facilities may require the observance of routine procedures before a guest speaker is invited to appear on campus, institutional control of campus facilities should never be used as a device of censorship. It should be made clear to the academic and larger community that sponsorship of guest speakers does not necessarily imply approval or endorsement of the views expressed, either by the sponsoring group or the institution.

C. *Student Participation in Institutional Government.* As constituents of the academic community, students should be free, individually and collectively, to express their views on issues of institutional policy and on matters of general interest to the student body. The student body should have clearly defined means to participate in the formulation and application of regulations affecting student affairs. Student governments should be protected from arbitrary intervention.

D. *Student Publications.* Student publications and the student press are a valuable aid in establishing and maintaining an atmosphere of free and responsible discussion and of intellectual exploration on the campus. They are a means of bringing student concerns to the attention of the faculty and the institutional authorities and of formulating student opinion on various issues on the campus and in the world at large.

1. The student press should be free of censorship and advance approval of copy, and its editors and managers should be free to develop their own editorial policies and news coverage.

2. The integrity and responsibility of student publications should be encouraged by arrangements which permit financial autonomy or, ideally, complete financial independence.

3. Editors and managers should subscribe to canons of responsible journalism. At the same time, they should be protected from arbitrary suspension and removal because of student, faculty, adminis-

trative, or public disapproval of editorial policy or content. Only for proper and stated causes should editors and managers be subject to removal and then by orderly and prescribed procedures.

IV. Off-Campus Freedom of Students

A. *Exercise of Rights of Citizenship.* As citizens, students should enjoy the same freedom of speech, peaceful assembly, and right of petition that other citizens enjoy. Faculty members and administrative officials should insure that institutional powers are not employed to inhibit such intellectual and personal development of students as is often promoted by their off-campus activities and their exercise of the rights of citizenship.

B. *Institutional Authority and Civil Penalities.* Activities of students may upon occasion result in violation of law. In such cases, institutional officials should apprise students of their legal rights and may offer other assistance. Students who violate the law may incur penalties prescribed by civil authorities, but institutional authority should never be used merely to duplicate the function of general laws. Only where the institution's interests as an academic community are distinct from those of the general community should the special authority of the institution be asserted. The student who incidentally violates institutional regulations in the course of his off-campus activity, such as those relating to class attendance, should be subject to no greater penalty than would normally be imposed. Institutional action should be independent of community pressure.

V. Procedural Standards in Disciplinary Proceedings

The disciplinary powers of educational institutions are inherent in their responsibility to protect their educational purpose through the regulation of the use of their facilities and through the setting of standards of conduct and scholarship for the students who attend them. In developing responsible student conduct, disciplinary proceedings play a role substantially secondary to counseling, guidance, admonition, and example. In the exceptional circumstances when these preferred means fail to resolve problems of student conduct, proper procedural safeguards should be observed to protect the student from the unfair imposition of serious penalties. The following are recommended as proper safeguards in such proceedings.[1]

A. *Notice of Standards of Conduct Expected of Students.* Disciplinary proceedings should be instituted only for violation of standards

[1] Honor codes offering comparable guarantees may be an acceptable substitute for the procedural standards set forth in this section.

of conduct defined in advance and published through such means as a student handbook or a generally available body of university regulations. Offenses should be as clearly defined as possible, and such vague phrases as "undesirable conduct" or "conduct injurious to the best interests of the institution" should be avoided. Conceptions of misconduct particular to the institution need clear and explicit definition.

B. *Investigation of Student Conduct.*

1. Except under emergency circumstances, premises occupied by students and the personal possessions of students should not be searched unless appropriate authorization has been obtained. For premises such as dormitories controlled by the institution, an appropriate and responsible authority should be designated to whom application should be made before a search is conducted. The application should specify the reasons for the search and the objects or information sought. The student should be present, if possible, during the search. For premises not controlled by the institution, the ordinary requirements for lawful search should be followed.

2. Students detected or arrested in the course of serious violations of institutional regulations, or infractions of ordinary law, should be informed of their rights. No form of harassment should be used by institutional representatives to coerce admissions of guilt or information about conduct of other suspected persons.

C. *Status of Student Pending Final Action.* Pending action on the charges, the status of a student should not be altered, or his right to be present on the campus and to attend classes suspended, except for reasons relating to his physical or emotional safety and well-being, or for reasons relating to the safety of students, faculty, or university property.

D. *Hearing Committee Procedures.* The formality of the procedure to which a student is entitled in disciplinary cases should be proportionate to the gravity of the offense and the sanctions which may be imposed. Minor penalties may be assessed informally under prescribed procedures. When misconduct may result in serious penalties, the student should have the right to a hearing before a regularly constituted hearing committee.

1. The hearing committee should include faculty members or, if regularly included or requested by the accused, both faculty and student members. No member of the hearing committee who is otherwise interested in the particular case should sit in judgment during the proceeding.

2. The student should be informed, in writing, of the reasons for

the proposed disciplinary action with sufficient particularity, and in sufficient time, to ensure opportunity to prepare for the hearing.

3. The student appearing before the hearing committee should have the right to be assisted in his defense by an adviser of his choice.

4. The burden of proof should rest upon the officials bringing the charge.

5. The student should be given an opportunity to testify and to present evidence and witnesses. He should have an opportunity to hear and question adverse witnesses. In no case should the committee consider statements against him unless he has been advised of their content and of the name of those who made them, and unless he has been given an opportunity to rebut unfavorable inferences which might otherwise be drawn.

6. All matters upon which the decision may be based must be introduced into evidence at the proceeding before the hearing committee. The decision should be based solely upon such matter. Improperly acquired evidence should not be admitted.

7. In the absence of a transcript, there should be both a digest and a verbatim record, such as a tape recording, of the hearing.

8. The decision of the hearing committee should be final, subject to the student's right of appeal to the governing board of the institution.

Appendix II

ACADEMIC FREEDOM AND CIVIL LIBERTIES OF STUDENTS IN COLLEGES AND UNIVERSITIES

AMERICAN CIVIL LIBERTIES UNION

INTRODUCTION

AMERICAN STUDENTS, like students in other countries, are participating increasingly in the political affairs of their society and are also seeking a larger voice in the determination of college policy. It is therefore appropriate for the American Civil Liberties Union to re-examine the various issues raised by this growing demand, and to state its own views regarding the proper freedom and responsibility of university and college students.*

The relationship between the educational institution and its students must be viewed in the light of the function of the college or university: to transmit to the student the civilization of the past, to enable him to take part in the civilization of the present and to make the civilization of the future.** In this great pursuit, the student must be viewed as an individual who is most likely to attain maturity if left free to make personal decisions and to exercise the rights, as well as shoulder the responsibilities, of citizenship on and off the campus.

I. THE COLLEGE, THE COMMUNITY AND THE EDUCATIONAL PROCESS

Like all complex human enterprises, the American college is made up of many groups—students, faculty, several levels of administration, and boards of trustees—which will at times disagree on means as well as goals. The college also exists in a network of human relations with many other organizations and constituencies, including alumni, par-

* As used in this pamphlet the word "college" refers to all institutions of higher education, including the university. The relevance of the principles and practices discussed, for students in secondary schools, is briefly set forth in Section VII, on page 203.

** Ralph Barton Perry, *Realms of Value*, Harvard University Press, 1954, p. 411.

ents, legislatures and various governmental agencies, which may desire to influence its policies.

The healthy, strong college asserts its autonomy, its necessary right to decide for itself, even though it is aware that many people constantly scrutinize its policies and can help or harm it by granting or with-holding support. The truly independent college will meet criticism not by modifying its policy, but by redoubling its efforts to persuade its constituencies that freedom is an important means toward its educational goal.

It is understandable that Boards of Trustees and Boards of Higher Education, to say nothing of college administrators themselves, should be acutely sensitive to public as well as private criticism. Yet it is clear that the *public* interest is not served when the *academic* community is fearful of experimentation, controversy and dissent.

The college which wishes to set an example of open-minded inquiry in its classrooms will defeat its purpose if it denies the same right of inquiry to its students outside the classroom—or if it imposes rules which deny them the freedom to make their own choices, wise or unwise. Limitations on the freedom of students are not then to be seen as simple administrative decisions which adjust the school to the prevailing climate of public opinion. The college's policy vis-a-vis its students goes to the heart of the condition necessary for adequate personal growth and thus determines whether an institution of higher education turns out merely graduates or the indispensable human material for a continuing democracy.

II. BASIC PRINCIPLES

A. FREEDOM OF EXPRESSION

The student government, student organizations, and individual students should be free to discuss, pass resolutions, distribute leaflets, circulate petitions, and take other lawful action respecting any matter which directly or indirectly concerns or affects them.

Students should take responsibility for helping to maintain a free academic community. They should respect and defend not only their fellow students' freedoms; but also their teachers' right to the free expression of views based on their own pursuit of the truth and their right to function as citizens, independently of the college or university.

B. FREEDOM FROM DISCRIMINATION

Just as the college should not discriminate on grounds of race, religion, color, or national origin in its admission policies, so should it not permit discrimination in any area of student life, such as housing on or off the campus, athletics, fraternities, social clubs, or other organizations.

C. GOVERNMENT BY LAW

Students should live under a government of law, created, where appropriate, by joint action of students, faculty and administration. The United States National Student Association has properly said: "The functioning of the educational community requires an awareness of mutual responsibility, understanding, trust, and respect in order that all its members actively contribute to the development of policies and programs; this purpose can best be achieved only through the continuous cooperation within the educational community. . . . These policies and procedures should in no case be subject to change without notice under the pressure of a particular situation, and the groups affected should participate at all times in their application."*

III. STUDENTS AS CAMPUS CITIZENS

A. STUDENT GOVERNMENT

The primary purpose of student government is to provide students with the means to regulate student-sponsored activities, organizations, publications and any other matters properly subject to their jurisdiction. The electorate of such a government should consist of the entire student body and should not be defined in terms of membership in clubs or organizations. Designation of delegates, officers, committees and boards should be by student vote only, should be non-discriminatory and should not be subject to administrative or faculty approval. Academic authorities may, however, set up a uniform and reasonable system of scholastic eligibility requirements for major student offices.

B. STUDENT CLUBS

1. *Freedom of Student Association:* Students should be free to organize and join associations for educational, political, social, religious or cultural purposes. The fact of affiliation with any extramural association or national organization or political party, so long as it is an open

* *Codification of Policy*, United States National Student Association, 1960–61, p. 25.

affiliation, should not of itself bar a group from recognition. Any campus group which plans political discussion or action within legal bounds should be allowed to organize in any educational institution. The administration should not discriminate against a student because of membership in any such organization.

2. *Registration and Disclosures:* A procedure for official recognition and registration of student organizations should be established by the student government. The organization applying for recognition should submit a constitution and provide information about its purposes, affiliations, officers and activities. Such information should be available to all within the college community and should be subject to publication on the campus. If a faculty-student committee has reason to believe that any organization has concealed, misrepresented, or otherwise failed to disclose its purposes or affiliations, it may require the organization to state or clarify them. Should such explanation not be forthcoming, the committee's findings may properly be publicized to the educational institution at large. Such a procedure has proved to be more effective from the educational standpoint than withdrawal of recognition or any other disciplinary action.

3. *Membership Lists:* Organizations should not be required to file a list of members, but, if number of students is a condition of chartering or financial aid, the club's officers and the faculty adviser may be required to attest to the fact of such numerically sufficient membership. The names of officers and members should not, without the consent of the individuals involved, be disclosed to any non-college person or organization or to any college persons having no direct and legitimate interest therein.

4. *Social clubs and fraternities* may be permitted to function provided they do not discriminate on grounds of race, religion, color, or national origin. For non-members, the college should provide living and eating facilities of as good a quality as those offered by fraternities or clubs.

5. *Use of Campus Facilities:* Meeting rooms and other campus facilities should be made available, as far as their primary use for educational purposes permits, on a non-discriminatory basis, to registered student organizations. Bulletin boards should be provided for the use of student organizations; school-wide circulation of all notices and leaflets which meet uniform and non-discriminatory standards should be permitted.

6. *Advisers for Organizations:* A student organization should be free to choose its own faculty adviser. No organization should be forbidden to function when, after reasonable effort, it has failed to obtain a faculty adviser. An adviser should consult with and advise the organization but should have no authority or responsibility to regulate or control its activities.

C. STUDENT-SPONSORED FORUMS

Students should be accorded the right to assemble, to select speakers and to discuss issues of their choice. When a student organization wishes to invite an outside speaker it should give sufficient notice to the college administration. The latter may properly inform the group's leaders of its views in the matter but should leave the final decision to them. Permission should not be withheld because the speaker is a controversial figure. It can be made clear to the public that an invitation to a speaker does not necessarily imply approval of his views by either the student group or the college administration. Students should enjoy the same right as other citizens to hear different points of view and draw their own conclusions. At the same time, faculty members and college administrators may if they wish acquaint students with the nature of organizations and causes that seek to enlist student support.

D. PAMPHLETS, PETITIONS AND DEMONSTRATIONS

Student organizations and individual students should be allowed, and no special permission should be required, to distribute pamphlets, except in classrooms and study halls, or collect names for petitions concerning either campus or off-campus issues. Orderly demonstrations on campus should not be prohibited.

E. STUDENT PUBLICATIONS

All student publications—college newspapers, literary and humor magazines, academic periodicals and yearbooks—should enjoy full freedom of the press. They are too often denied it by college administrations which fear public criticism. Except for the relatively few university dailies which are independent financially, college publications in general are dependent on the administration's favor in that they use campus facilities and are subsidized either directly by the college or indirectly by a tax on student funds.

The College Newspaper: Whether a daily or a weekly, the campus paper should report news of student interest on and off campus, should provide an outlet for student and faculty opinion through letters to the editor, and make its own editorial comments on college and other matters. While these comments need not necessarily represent the view of the majority of students, fair space should be given to dissenting opinion.

The advisory board of the college newspaper, or college publications board which supervises all student publications, should be composed of at least a majority of students, selected by the student government or council or by some other democratic method. Other members might include a member of the faculty of the School of Journalism in universities with such schools, an alumnus, a local newspaper editor, or other qualified citizen, and such representation from the liberal arts faculty and/or Dean's office as may be mutually agreed upon.

One of the main duties of the publications or advisory board may be the interviewing of qualified candidates and the selection of the editor-in-chief and possibly of all the major staff writers on the campus newspaper. In colleges where this is not the practice, some other method of selection, appropriate to the institution, should be devised by the student government to ensure that competent responsible editors are put in charge and that the college newspaper does not fall into the hands of a self-perpetuating clique.

The editor-in-chief should be left free to exercise his own best judgment in the selection of material to be published. The adults on the board (or the faculty adviser if the paper has a single consultant) should counsel the editors in the ethics and responsibilities of journalism, but neither a faculty member nor an administrator should exercise veto power over what may be printed. Should the board as a whole, after publication, consider that the paper's editor has exercised excessively poor judgment, in one or a number of instances, it may take steps to impeach and remove him from office, after holding hearings and according him due process rights.

Literary and Humor Magazines: Since the literary magazine, in common with other student academic periodicals in such fields as the social sciences, the humanities, the natural sciences, economics, etc., is an extension of classroom activity, students should be as free in writing for and editing such a magazine as in submitting papers to their instructors or in making comments in class. The same freedom of expression should be accorded the college humor magazine. Whether such magazines are responsible to a college publications board or have a single faculty adviser, chosen by the editors, they should be accorded the same freedom to print as the college newspaper. While adult sensibilities may at times be offended by youthful humor and lack of taste, a policy of encouraging the editors to use their best judgment places the responsibility where it belongs, on the editor and not on the college administration. In the long run the editor's product will be accepted or rejected by student readers.

In summary, the college administration which takes no step to control the content of a student publication, and refrains, in a controversial situation, from suspending or discontinuing publication or penalizing one or more student editors, testifies to its belief in the principles of academic freedom and freedom of the press. The student governing body, for its part, should encourage a sufficiently large number of able, responsible and interested students to seek editorial and writing positions, and should devise appropriate selection procedures if they do not already exist.*

F. RADIO AND TELEVISION

College radio and TV stations whose signal goes beyond the campus operate under a license granted by the Federal Communications Commission and are therefore responsible to the government as well as to the college administration which provides the facilities. Since the law requires that "the public interest, convenience and necessity" be served, all radio and TV stations are obligated to present all sides of controversial issues. Also, under an FCC ruling of 1949, all stations are free to editorialize in the name of the station provided they make answering time available to responsible opponents. While campus, like other radio and TV stations, accordingly enjoy under the law broad freedom of speech, they are forbidden by the Federal Communications Act to broadcast "profane or obscene words, language, or meaning." Inasmuch as radio and TV are a family medium, literary or humorous material which student editors may think suitable to print might be considered an infringement on the FCC law.

* In summarizing replies to a questionnaire on *Supervision and Control of Student Publications*, sent to 127 colleges and answered by 105, John E. Hocutt, Dean of Students at the University of Delaware, writes, "The three points made most often by those commenting are the difficulty of finding interested, qualified faculty to serve as advisers to student publications; the need to improve the fiscal operation of student publications; and the scarcity of interested, able students who seek top editorial positions." University of Delaware, Office of the Dean of Students, Newark, Delaware, March, 1961, mimeo. 15 pp.

On campuses where the radio or TV station is used as a closely-linked teaching adjunct by such departments as drama, speech and communications, faculty direction becomes necessary.

Student directors of campus communications stations which are not used primarily for instruction, after being counseled by the college administration in their responsibility to the FCC and to the public, should thereafter be granted, within legal limits, the same freedom of judgment and action as should editors of college publications. The same freedom should be accorded to student directors of closed-circuit stations which reach only campus listeners and are not used primarily for instruction.

IV. Regulations Concerning Student Life and Discipline

A. ENACTMENT AND PROMULGATION OF REGULATIONS

Responsibility for regulations on academic matters naturally rests with the faculty and administration. Regulations governing the conduct of students should be enacted by a committee composed of students, administrators and faculty members if desired.

Regulations governing the behavior of students should be fully and clearly formulated, published, and made available to the whole academic community. They should be reasonable and realistic. Overelaborate rules that seek to govern student conduct in every detail tend either to be respected in the breach, or to hinder the development of mature attitudes. As a rule, specific definitions are preferable to such general criteria as "conduct unbecoming to a student" or "against the best interests of the institution," which allow for a wide latitude of interpretation.

B. DUE PROCESS IN DISCIPLINARY CASES

In most institutions the faculty joins the administration in making and enforcing the regulations for the disciplining of students for academic derelictions including cheating. Failure to meet academic standards is patently a ground for probation or dismissal. But since a student expelled for cheating may find it difficult or impossible to continue his academic career, he should be protected by every procedural safeguard. This is particularly necessary since the courts have rarely granted the student legal review or redress; they have assumed that the academic institution itself is in the best position to judge culpability. This places the college in the unique position of being prosecutor and judge and having at the same time the moral obligation to serve as a trustee of the student's welfare.

No student should be expelled or suffer major disciplinary action for any offense, other than failure to meet the required academic standards, without having been advised explicitly of the charges against him, which at his request should be in writing. He should be free to seek the counsel of a faculty member of his choice or other adviser. Should he admit guilt but consider the penalty excessive, or should he claim to be innocent, he may ask for a hearing by a review committee. After ample notice, such a hearing should be held by a faculty-student committee, or if the student prefers, by a faculty committee. The hearing committee should examine the evidence, hear witnesses as to the facts and the student's character, and weigh extenuating circumstances. The student should be allowed to call witnesses on his own behalf and confront and cross-examine those who appear against him. If the review committee's decision as to the student's innocence or guilt and in the latter case, appropriate punishment, is not acceptable to the college administration, a final appeal to the board of trustees should be allowed.

V. Students as Private Citizens

A. NON-ACADEMIC ACTIVITIES

In their non-academic life, private or public, students should be free from college control. On the other hand, the college should not be held responsible for the non-academic activities of its individual students.

The student, like the teacher, is a member not only of an academic community, but of the community at large and of other specific communities. His college must regard him as both a student and a private individual. It must recognize that his being a student is sometimes irrelevant to his private status. In this private status he should not be subject to punitive measures by the college, unless the college can prove (in the course of a hearing with due process safeguards as specified in IV) that he has acted in a way which adversely affects or seriously interferes with its normal educational function, or which injures or endangers the welfare of any of its other members.

B. OFF-CAMPUS ACTIVITIES

No disciplinary action should be taken by college against a student for engaging in such off-campus activities as political campaigns, picketing, or participating in public demonstrations, provided the student does not claim without authorization to speak or act in the name of the college or one of its student organizations. Students should observe the same kind of self-discipline that their teachers accept when they speak as citizens and not as representatives of their educational institution.

When students choose to participate in activities that result in police action, such as demonstrations against segregation, the civilian defense program or nuclear tests, it is an infringement of their liberty for the college to punish such activity. Students who violate a local ordinance or any law which they consider to be morally wrong, risk the legal penalties prescribed by the civilian authorities. Since not every conviction under law is for an offense with which an educational institution must concern itself, it is incumbent on the college to refrain from administrative decisions which would violate the students' academic freedom.

In this connection, it is important to make clear that our discussion here concerns convictions. A record of mere arrest, not followed by conviction, should not be used by any educational institution to penalize a student in any way. As is any other citizen, a student is presumed to be innocent until proven otherwise.

And even in the case of conviction of a student for civil rights and other political activities such as those listed in paragraph (B) above, this should be distinguished by the college from convictions for criminal offenses not involving First Amendment considerations. In screening candidates for admission, college officials should take the position that the existence of an arrest or conviction record for civil rights and other political activities is irrelevant to the question of admission. However, even where the practice is to take cognizance of such records, this inclusion should not be permitted to affect adversely the student's chances of admission.

When students run into police difficulties off the campus in connection with what they regard as their political rights—as, for example, taking part in sit-ins, picket lines, demonstrations, riding on freedom buses—the college authorities should take every practical step to assure themselves that such students are protected in their full legal rights, to wit: That they are given fair trials in a court of law where they are defended by counsel. That they are not abused by the police and that charges are brought against the police if the latter act wrongfully. That bail be sought and furnished. That they have speedy trials and that appeals be taken when necessary. Ideally, the college itself should provide such assistance. If this is not feasible, then the administration should permit and encourage individual faculty, student or alumni groups to render the help required.

In order to protect the interests of students convicted for civil rights and other political activities, a college should separate the records of such convictions from other student records. In other words, such records ought to be given a restricted status in order to obviate intentional or unintentional abuse. In order further to protect the interests of students, an institution should not make the records in question available to prospective employers, graduate and professional schools, or government agencies, without the consent of students involved.

Unless college authorities act in behalf of students, there is the very real danger of alienation: of the weakening of confidence in the university as a community and the resort by students to outside agencies —some of which may very well be self-serving—for support and defense. College authorities have as much responsibility for maintaining that community—based upon mutual trust, respect, and forbearance—as do teachers and students.

Both the United States Civil Service Commission and all similar state commissions require applicants to answer a question regarding arrests or convictions for any offense other than minor traffic violations. Although we believe mere arrest records should not be used to penalize applicants, a student should answer such a question fully and accurately. Where the interrogation, arrest or conviction occurs as the result of civil rights and civil liberties activities, he should make it a point to specify in detail the circumstances, including the kind of court before which such a hearing took place. In this connection, the philosophy of the United States Civil Service Commission, as expressed in a letter to the ACLU from Chairman John W. Macy, Jr., dated May 12, 1964, is commended for the consideration of state and local commissions although we continue to believe that all references to "arrests" should be replaced by "convictions."

> "When the information furnished indicates that the arrest was in connection with a peaceful demonstration for civil rights or similar purposes, the arrest is not used by the Commission as a basis for disqualifying the applicant. When the arrest was for a more serious offense than peaceful demonstration for civil rights or similar purposes, it is considered on its individual merits in terms of the specific circumstances involved.

"The Commission has a sincere concern that civil rights arrests not be used arbitrarily to disqualify applicants. Accordingly we have instructed our regional offices to submit to us for approval any cases in which they consider the circumstances so serious as to warrant adverse action. Our purpose in doing this is to assure review of these cases at the highest level of responsibility."

C. TEACHER DISCLOSURE*

Teachers who are asked to supply information to employers or prospective employers, governmental or private, about students or former students should be aware of the dangers to academic freedom inherent in this proliferating practice. Since the best education calls for probing, sharing and hypothesizing, and for uninhibited expression and thinking out loud by the student, disclosure by the teacher to a source outside the college community of a student's expressed opinion, or the making of a statement based on such an opinion, becomes a threat to the educational process.

The teacher-student relation is a privileged one. The student does not normally expect that either his utterances in the classroom, or his discussions with teachers outside the classroom, or his written views, will be reported beyond the walls of the college community. If he knew that anything he said or wrote might be revealed indiscriminately, the kind of relation in which he originally felt free to voice his thoughts, would cease to exist. While no detailed prescription can be set down for teachers, who must remain free to use their own judgment, the following standards, with the reasons therefore, are recommended:

When interrogated directly by prospective employers of any kind, public or private, or indirectly by the institution's administrative officers in behalf of prospective employers, a teacher can safely answer questions which he finds clearly concerned with the student's competence and fitness for the job. There is always the chance that even questions of this kind will covertly require the teacher to violate academic privacy. Questions and answers in written form make it easier to avoid pitfalls, but the teacher's alertness is always essential. Ordinarily, questions relating to what the student has demonstrated as a student—for example, the ability to write in a certain way, to solve problems of a certain kind, to reason consistently, to direct personnel or other projects—pose no threat to educational privacy. But, ques-

* Reprint available from the ACLU of full statement on "Teacher Disclosure," adopted by the Academic Freedom Committee and printed in *School and Society*, October 7, 1961. *Five cents per copy.*

tions relating to the student's loyalty and patriotism, his political or religious or moral or social beliefs and attitudes, his general outlook, his private life, may if answered jeopardize the teacher-student relation.

As a safeguard against the danger of putting the student in an unfavorable light with government representatives or employers of any category, simply as a result of the fact that some questions are answerable and others are not, teachers can preface each questionnaire with a brief *pro forma* statement that the academic policy to which they subscribe makes it inadvisable to answer certain types of questions. Once this academic policy becomes widespread, presumptive inferences about individual students will no longer be made by employers.

Whether or not the student wishes his teacher in a given instance to disclose details which adherence to general academic principles would leave undisclosed, is irrelevant. Personal expediency of this kind has uncertain consequences and does not seem justifiable as an exception to warranted policy. This choice again involves a balancing of risks. An individual student might benefit from having his teacher answer questions about him fully; yet a satisfactory principle would not admit *ad hoc* violations of academic sanctuary.

It is to be hoped that faculty senates or other representative faculty bodies will take cognizance of the teacher disclosure problem, and will recommend action which would leave intact the teacher-student relationship.

D. HOUSING

Wherever numbers of students are obliged to live off-campus because of insufficient dormitory space, or because they are married, the college administration should ensure that private rentals are on a non-discriminatory basis.*

VI. STUDENTS IN SCHOOLS BELOW THE COLLEGE LEVEL

Considerable progress has been made in extending the principles of free student expression and association to American secondary schools.

* A study published in 1961 by the New York State Commission Against Discrimination revealed that only 19 out of more than 100 colleges and universities surveyed across the country in 1959 reported having regulations which forbid bias in renting to students. *Housing Bias in the College Community*, N.Y. State Commission Against Discrimination, N.Y.C. 7, 1961, mimeo, 10 pp.

A good secondary school usually has a student government democratically organized, with a clear budget of power. In the secondary school, student publications should provide as much opportunity as possible for the sincere expression of all shades of student opinion. Traditionally, principals have a legal veto over student activities, but the wise principal in an enlightened community uses this veto seldom and with great reluctance, and explains his reasons carefully. Most American schools include among their educational objectives the development of civic competence, and an acceptance of a responsibility for active participation in the civic affairs of a free society. The imposition of loyalty oaths, arbitrary punishment for editorials on controversial issues, or for participation in orderly demonstrations supporting such causes as integration or nuclear disarmament or in protest against the civilian defense program, will tend to make the objecting students at once cynical and resentful, and the student body as a whole conformist. In rating students for college admission, principals and teachers should not down-grade those who have shown independence of spirit in promoting such activities. It is further recommended that in supplying information about former students to government investigators and private employers, high school principals and faculty members answer no "questions relating to the student's loyalty and patriotism, his political or religious or moral or social beliefs and attitudes, his general outlook and his private life."*

The principles set forth in this pamphlet on "Academic Freedom and Civil Liberties of Students in Colleges and Universities" are consistent with those expressed by many leading educators. President James F. Dixon of Antioch College, after a group of students had staged an off-campus demonstration against a governmental action, commented as follows in the May 1961 edition of *Antioch Notes:*

> ". . . the college as a total community does not take positions on political matters that are local or international. Our business is education, not politics. But this does not mean that we restrict the positions that members of the faculty or members of the student body may take on social and political concerns.

> "As a matter of fact we believe that academic freedom is as important to the student as it is for the faculty member. We recognize that these kinds of activities by students are widely interpreted and, we believe, sometimes misinterpreted in the community. They are misinterpreted because they are not

* See page 199 above.

understood to be part of an educational process. They are misinterpreted because, not understood as part of an educational process, they are regarded as irresponsible kinds of actions.

"But I think it is important to recognize that these activities are part of the total educational process that we have in our colleges, and that these are the young people who are going to be deeply involved in the political and social affairs of the next decade; that wise people believe that the problems of the next decade require us to develop leadership with sufficient courage to take positions, that one of the ways in which one learns how to do this is by doing it, and that there should be an opportunity in the educational situation to do this in a fashion that is, shall I say, somewhat experimental. . . ."

Delineating the university's over-all function, Dean Erwin N. Griswold of the Harvard Law School wrote in 1961:

"A university is the place where students learn not merely from the past but also through developing the capacity for and habit of independent thought. If they are well taught, they learn to do their own thinking. There is no 'party line' in any American university worthy of the name. Great ideas can rarely be developed in an atmosphere of constraint and oppression. The university has a unique function not merely in systematizing the orthodox, but also in providing the soil in which may be nourished the speculative, the unfashionable, and the unorthodox. . . ."*

In common with these educators and others of their persuasion, the American Civil Liberties Union and its Academic Freedom Committee believe that today's young people, who will be responsible in the not too distant future for the conduct of the Nation's political and social affairs, will have been ill-prepared unless they have as students developed "the capacity for and habit of independent thought."

* Griswold, Hesburgh, Sachar and Everett. *The Challenge to American Education*, Anti-Defamation League, 515 Madison Avenue, N.Y.C. 22, 1961, pg. 15.

BIBLIOGRAPHY

The following bibliography lists books published in or since 1964 which are relevant to the problems of freedom and order in universities. Brief descriptions of the books are provided. For earlier works, see *Selected Issues in Higher Education: An Annotated Bibliography* (L. R. Meeth, ed., Teacher's College, Columbia University, 1965), which provides two hundred pages of references to books and articles published from about 1950 to 1965. Among the subject divisions are "Technological and Social Pressures Affecting the Future of Higher Education," "Higher Educational Institutions as Social Organisms," "Public Relations in Higher Education," and "Student Participation in College Policy Formulation and Administration."

Airan, Judson William, *College Administration: A Proposal.* Taplinger, 1966. Changes occurring in college administration in India in order to increase student and faculty participation within the framework of university and government regulations.

Baskin, Samuel, ed., *Higher Education: Some Newer Developments.* McGraw-Hill, 1965. Papers by educators and researchers on the advantages, limitations, and problems of higher education.

Bell, Daniel, *The Reforming of General Education.* Columbia University Press, 1965. Comparison of undergraduate curricula, with specific attention to Columbia College, Chicago, and Harvard.

Benson, Charles S., *The Cheerful Prospect: A Statement on the Future of American Education.* Houghton Mifflin, 1965. Suggests changes in the ways of financing and administering schools so as to make educational favoritism impossible.

Bergen, Dan, and Duryea, E. D., eds., *Libraries and the College Climate.* Syracuse University Press, 1966. Six essays on the relationship between campus educational programs and the college library.

Berkner, L .V., *The Scientific Age: The Impact of Science on Society.* Yale University Press, 1964. The relationship of higher education and economic growth in contemporary society.

Brameld, Theodore, and Elam, Stanley, eds., *Values in American Education: An Interdisciplinary Approach.* Phi Delta Kappa, 1964. Five essays and supporting discussion from a symposium sponsored by the educational honorary fraternity.

Brickman, William W., and Lehrer, Stanley, *Automation, Education, and Human Values.* Society for the Advancement of Education, 1966. Essays on the effects of technological change and related issues in education.

Brookover, Wilbur B., *et al.*, *The College Student.* Center for Applied Research in Education, 1965. Sociological study of student character and culture.

Brubacher, John S., *Basis for Policy in Higher Education.* McGraw-Hill, 1965. Comparison of the views of Newman, Veblen, Ortega y Gasset, Hutchins, and others on higher education.

Burns, Gerald P., *Trustees in Higher Education: Their Functions and Coordinations.* Independent College Funds of America, 1966. The governmental structure of colleges and universities as it is and as it ought to be.

Campbell, Angus, and Eckerman, William C., *Public Concepts of the Values and Costs of Higher Education.* University of Michigan Press, 1965. A national survey of public opinion on the cost, income, and status of a college education; its importance to the individual and society; and the financial problems of institutions of higher education.

Carter, Allan M., *An Assessment of Quality in Graduate Education.* American Council on Education, 1966. Comparison of scholarly reputation of faculty and effectiveness of doctoral programs at 106 American universities.

Chambers, M. M., *The Colleges and the Courts Since 1950.* Interstate, 1964. Higher state and federal court decisions regarding racial desegregation, the loyalty oath, taxes and finances of public and private institutions.

Chambers, M. M., *Freedom and Repression in Higher Education.* Bloomcraft, 1965. Papers on the purposes of higher education and the financing of public higher education, and a critique of Conant's *Shaping Educational Policy.*

Cohen, Joseph W., ed., *The Superior Student in American Higher Education.* McGraw-Hill, 1966. Honors students and honors programs in the context of their historic development.

Cohen, Mitchell, and Hale, Dennis, eds., *The New Student Left*. Beacon, 1966. A comprehensive expression of the young campus radicals' rejection of national values and policies.

Conant, James B., *Shaping Educational Policy*. McGraw-Hill, 1964. An examination of the policy-making bodies in American education and the need for a nation-wide policy.

———, *Two Modes of Thought: My Encounters with Science and Education*. Trident, 1964. An exploration of the interplay between the empirical-inductive method of inquiry and the theoretical-deductive method as they are employed in research and education.

Cremin, Lawrence A., *The Genius of American Education*. University of Pittsburgh Press, 1965. A well-known educator discusses American education and its relation to democratic principles.

Curti, Merle, and Nash, Roderick, *Philanthropy in the Shaping of American Higher Education*. Rutgers University Press, 1965. The impact of private giving on the differences between American and European higher education, on the founding of women's and Negro colleges, and on quality and innovation in education.

Dadson, D. F., ed., *On Higher Education*. University of Toronto Press, 1966. Diverse approaches to the conduct of university affairs.

Danière, André, *Higher Education in the American Economy*. Random House, 1964. Analyzes education as consumer goods, discusses the non-monetary cultural benefits, and suggests solutions to the problem of providing public higher education to those who cannot afford it.

Dennis, Lawrence E., and Kauffman, Joseph F., eds., *The College and the Student*. American Council on Education, 1965. Papers by college presidents, deans, professors, and students on student rights, freedoms, and responsibilities; the moral revolution; and student-faculty-administration conflict.

DeVane, William, *Higher Education in Twentieth Century America*. Harvard University Press, 1965. An interpretation of the current difficulties in colleges and universities in historical perspective.

Dober, Richard, *The New Campus in Britain: Ideas of Consequence for the United States*. Educational Facilities Laboratories, 1965. Reviews the master plans of eight British universities.

Draper, Hal, *Berkeley: The New Student Revolt*. Evergreen, 1965. An account of the Berkeley incident by a participant, with selections from items published by students, faculty, administration, and regents at the time of the revolt.

Education at Berkeley. Report of the Berkeley Faculty Senate. University of California Press, 1965. An analysis of student unrest and proposals for improvement of undergraduate and graduate instruction. (Known as the Muscatine Report.)

Friedenberg, Edgar, *Growth and Acquiescence: Coming of Age in America*. Random House, 1965. A study of how adolescents react when asked to choose between opposing values—the private values of excellence or the public values of effective socialization.

Friedman, Albert B., ed., *Creativity in Graduate Education*. Claremont Graduate School, 1965. Addresses by Milton S. Eisenhower, Louis T. Benezet, and Robert R. Sears.

Goodman, Paul, *Compulsory Mis-education*. Horizon, 1964. Criticism of current educational standards from primary grades through college, with recommendations for change.

The Graduate Study of Education. Report of the Harvard Committee on the Graduate Study of Education. Harvard University Press, 1966. A committee from the Faculty of Education considers how the graduate study of education should be viewed in a strong independent university.

Gross, Ronald, and Murphy, Judith, eds., *The Revolution in the Schools*. Harcourt, Brace and World, 1964. Essays on new departures in education.

Harris, Seymour E., ed., *Challenge and Change in American Education*. McCutchan, 1965. Papers and discussion from a seminar at the Harvard Graduate School of Public Administration.

————, ed., *Education and Public Policy*. McCutchan, 1965. Proceedings of a seminar at Harvard Graduate School of Public Administration.

Hettlinger, Richard, *Living with Sex: The Students' Dilemma*. Seabury, 1965. The problems of the college student in an era of changing standards of sexual behavior.

Hungate, Thad L., *Management in Higher Education*. Teachers College, Columbia University, 1964. Administration in relation to changing social institutions.

Husain, Zakir, *The Dynamic University*. Taplinger, 1965. Addresses by the vice-president of India examining the need for reorienting higher education to suit national needs in a developing country.

Huus, Helen, ed., *Freedom and Education*. University of Pennsylvania Press, 1965. The proceedings of the Annual Schoolmen Week, 1963.

Inlow, Gail M., *The Emergent in Curriculum*. Wiley, 1966. Assesses recent curriculum changes, advocating development of the total personality and opposing neglect of the humanities.

Jacobs, Paul, and Landau, Saul, *The New Radicals: A Report with Documents*. Random House, 1966. Analytical examination of the young radical activists who have repudiated traditional liberalism and who seek a new vision of America through civil rights work, university reform, and antiwar and antipoverty activities.

Jones, William C., ed., *Higher Education for All?* Oregon State University Press, 1965. Proceedings of the 1965 Pacific Northwest Conference on Higher Education.

Johnston, Bernard, ed., *Issues in Education*. Houghton Mifflin, 1964. Classical and contemporary selections on teaching as a profession, academic freedom, methodology, and the ideals of education.

Katope, Christopher G., and Zobrod, Paul G., eds., *Beyond Berkeley: A Sourcebook of Student Values*. World, 1965. Magazine articles on the Berkeley incident, with classical and contemporary essays on the history, purposes, and control of universities.

Keats, John, *The Sheepskin Psychosis*. Lippincott, 1965. Discusses the problems of higher education as raised in interviews with students, parents, and college officials.

Keenan, Boyd R., ed., *Science and the University*. Columbia University Press, 1965. Report of a symposium at Purdue University on the problems of teaching versus research, the use of federal money in the university, and the extent to which the university should develop independent research activities.

Keniston, Kenneth, *The Uncommitted*. Harcourt, Brace and World, 1965. A study of a small number of extremely alienated Harvard undergraduates.

Keppel, Francis, *The Necessary Revolution in American Education*. Harper and Row, 1966. An interpretation of the current problems in education and a demand for improvement in the quality of education.

King, Arthur R., and Brownell, John A., *The Curriculum and the Disciplines of Knowledge*. Wiley, 1965. A theory of curriculum based on a "communities of discourse" model of the disciplines of knowledge.

Klotsche, Martin J., *The Urban University*. Harper and Row, 1965. The problems and the potential of institutions of higher education in an urban setting.

Lineberry, William P., ed., *Colleges at the Crossroads*. Wilson, 1966. Articles on the historical development of the modern American college, the critical problems of higher education, the personality of today's college student, and the problems of faculty members.

Lipset, Seymour Martin, and Wolin, Sheldon S., eds., *The Berkeley Student Revolt*. Doubleday Anchor, 1965. A detailed chronology of events, and comments by participants and observers.

Luce, Phillip Abbott, *The New Left*. McKay, 1966. A former leader in the New Left movement denounces student rebels as dupes of the Communists and potential revolutionaries.

Machlup, Fritz, *The Production and Distribution of Knowledge in the United States*. Princeton University Press, 1966. Analysis of the "knowledge industries" and their contributions to the growth and spread of knowledge.

Mallery, David, *Ferment on Campus*. Harper and Row, 1965. Survey of college student attitudes which focuses on the dynamics of political and social action.

Martin, Boyd A., ed., *Responsibilities of Colleges and Universities*. Oregon State University Press, 1966. Papers presented at the 1966 Pacific Northwest Conference on Higher Education.

McGrath, Earl J., *The Predominantly Negro Colleges and Universities in Transition*. Teachers College, Columbia University, 1965. The present status, needs, and functions of Negro colleges.

————, ed., *Universal Higher Education*. McGraw-Hill, 1966. Twelve papers on the personal, institutional, and social implications of universal higher education.

Meeth, L. Richard, ed., *Selected Issues in Higher Education*. Teachers College, Columbia University, 1965. See above, p. 207.

Meredith, James H., *Three Years in Mississippi*. Indiana University Press, 1966. The first Negro to attend the University of Mississippi describes his experiences there.

Miller, Michael V., and Gilmore, Susan, eds., *Revolution at Berkeley: The Crisis in American Education*. Dial, 1965. Collection of articles, pamphlets, and newspaper accounts about the demonstrations at Berkeley and the ensuing debate over what a university should be.

Morison, Robert S., ed., *The Contemporary University: USA*. Houghton Mifflin, 1965. Essays by scholars and administrators on some of the perplexing problems arising on campuses today. A *Daedalus* Library edition.

Newman, Jack, *A Prophetic Minority*. New American Library, 1966. A collection of articles from the *Village Voice* discussing the New Left, distinquishing it from the Hereditary Left, and concentrating on the Students for a Democratic Society.

Niblett, W. R., ed., *The Expanding University*. Verry, 1966. Record of a conference held in Oxford by university teachers speaking from the Christian point of view on the role of the university.

Non-Western Studies in the Liberal Arts College. A report of the Commission on International Understanding, Association of American Colleges, 1964. Problems involved in incorporating a systematic study of the non-Western world into a liberal arts curriculum.

Perkins, James A., *The University in Transition*. Princeton University Press, 1965. An examination of the paradoxes of the university by the president of Cornell.

Pervin, Lawrence A., Reik, Louis E., and Dalrymple, Willard, *The College Dropout and the Utilization of Talent*. Princeton University Press, 1966. Examines factors that influence the decision to leave school and investigates ways to encourage the resumption of studies.

Peterson, Alexander Duncan Campbell, *A Hundred Years of Education*. Humanities, 1965. Comparative survey of developments and educational philosophy in Europe and the United States.

Raushenbush, Esther, *The Student and His Studies*. Wesleyan University Press, 1964. Detailed analysis of the intellectual development of four college students from their freshman year to graduation.

Read, Sir Herbert Edward, *The Redemption of the Robot: My Encounter with Education Through Art*. Trident, 1966. Expresses the opinion that present educational systems are turning people into robots by suppressing imagination and morality.

Reeves, Marjorie, ed., *Eighteen Plus: Unity and Diversity in Higher Education*. Humanities, 1966. Essay on many aspects of higher education and the student experience.

Ross, Murray G., ed., *New Universities in the Modern World*. St Martin's, 1965. Reports of presidents or vice-chancellors on the founding of ten new universities in seven countries.

Rudy, Willis, *Schools in an Age of Mass Culture*. Prentice-Hall, 1965. The forces, institutions, and educational theories that reflect the impact of an evolving mass society on a system of democratic education.

Russell, James E., *Change and Challenge in American Education*. Houghton Mifflin, 1965. The changes in the philosophical context of American education and how the different levels of education are responding to this challenge.

Sanford, Nevitt, ed., *College and Character*. Wiley, 1965. Critical studies of all the facets of college life by educators.

Sex and the College Student. A report of the Committee on the College Student, Group for the Advancement of Psychiatry. Atheneum, 1965. Analyzes sexual behavior on the campus with guidelines for administrative policy and understanding.

Sloman, Albert E., *A University in the Making.* Oxford University Press, 1964. BBC Lectures on the planning and establishing of the new University of Essex, by its vice-chancellor.

Stickler, W. Hugh, ed., *Experimental Colleges: Their Role in American Higher Education.* Florida State University Press, 1964. Report of a colloquium describing the aims, structure, and accomplishments of eleven participating schools.

Stroup, Herbert, *Toward a Philosophy of Organized Student Activities.* University of Minnesota Press, 1964. How student activities, given the proper objectives and means of realizing them, can contribute greatly to the educational process.

Stroup, Thomas Bradley, *The University in the American Future.* University of Kentucky Press, 1966. Papers presented at a conference on higher education.

Tannenbaum, F., ed., *A Community of Scholars.* Praeger, 1965. History and critique of the University Seminars founded at Columbia in 1944 to foster interdisciplinary cooperation.

Taylor, Herbert G., Jr., ed., *New Knowledge: Its Impact on Higher Education.* Oregon State University Press, 1965. Papers presented at the 1964 Pacific Northwest Conference on Higher Education.

The Troubled Campus. Atlantic–Little, Brown, 1966. Articles originally appearing in the *Atlantic Monthly*, written by students, professors, and administrators.

Ulich, Robert, ed., *Education and the Idea of Mankind.* Harcourt, Brace and World, 1964. Essay built around the theme that the unity of mankind offers a basis for liberal education.

The University Looks Abroad: Approaches to World Affairs at Six American Universities. Walker, 1965. Reports from Stanford, Michigan State, Tulane, Wisconsin, Cornell, and Indiana on the nature and extent of their involvement in world affairs.

van Hoffman, Nicholas, *The Multiversity: A Personal Report on What Happens to Today's Students in American Universities.* Holt, Rinehart and Winston, 1966. A discussion, largely in dialogue form, of many of the inadequacies of contemporary American university life.

Walters, Everett, ed., *Graduate Education Today.* American Council on Education, 1965. Essays on graduate education by past and present graduate deans.

Warshaw, Steven, *The Trouble in Berkeley*. Diablo Press, 1966. The history of the student rebellion in text and pictures.

Williams, Robert L., *The Administration of Academic Affairs in Higher Education*. The University of Michigan Press, 1965. The relation of administrative policies and procedures to the academic functions and achievements of higher education.

Wilson, Logan, ed., *Emerging Patterns in American Higher Education*. American Council on Education, 1965. Papers from the annual meeting of the American Council on Education in 1964.

Zinn, Howard, *SNCC: The New Abolitionists*. Beacon, 1964. An account of the activities of the Student Non-violent Coordinating Committee in behalf of racial equality in the South.

ABOUT THE CONTRIBUTORS

Samuel Gorovitz was born in Boston in 1938. He received his B.S. from the Massachusetts Institute of Technology in 1960, and his Ph.D. from Stanford University in 1963. During 1963–64 he taught at Wayne State University; since then he has been at Western Reserve University, where he is currently Assistant Professor of Philosophy in the WRU-Case Program of Philosophical Studies. His publications include items in *The Philosophical Review, The Journal of Philosophy, Philosophy of Science,* and *Medical Research Engineering.* He is co-author of *Philosophical Analysis: An Introduction to Its Language and Techniques.*

Paul Goodman was born in New York City in 1911. He received his B.A. from the City College of New York in 1931, and his Ph.D. (the work for which was completed in 1940) was awarded by the University of Chicago in 1954. He has taught at the University of Chicago and at Black Mountain College, has worked as a psychotherapist, was the 1964 Knapp Distinguished Scholar in Urban Affairs at the University of Wisconsin, conducts seminars at the Institute for Policy Studies in Washington, D.C., and is widely known for his lectures and writings in many fields. His scholarly works include *The Structure of Literature* and *Kafka's Prayer;* his novels include *The Empire City* and *Making Do;* and his plays include *Jonah* and *The Young Disciple.* But he is best known for his works of social criticism, including *Growing Up Absurd, People or Personnel, Compulsory Mis-education,* and *The Community of Scholars.*

Walter P. Metzger was born in New York City in 1922. He received his B.S.S. from the City College of New York in 1942, his M.A. from Columbia University in 1945, and his Ph.D. from the State University of Iowa in 1950. From 1947 to 1950 he was instructor at the State University of Iowa; he then moved to Columbia, where he is now Professor of History. He has been a Fellow of the Salzburg Seminar, and was a Fellow at the Center for Advanced Studies in the Behavioral Sciences in 1956–57. His many publications include items in *Philosophy of Science,* the *Antioch Review,* and the *University of Chicago Law Review.* In addition to contributing frequently to the *American Association of University Professors Bulletin,* he has served as co-editor of *American Non-Fiction, 1900–1950,* has written articles for a number of anthologies, is co-author of *Development of Academic Freedom in the United States,* and is author of *Academic Freedom in the Age of the University.*

John R. Searle was born in Denver in 1932. He attended the University of Wisconsin and was a Rhodes Scholar at Oxford University. He received baccalaureate and doctoral degrees from Oxford, and taught there as a Lecturer in Philosophy in Christ Church College. He has been a member of the faculty of the University of California at Berkeley since 1959, taught at the University of Michigan in 1961–62, and was a Fellow of the American Council of Learned Societies at the Massachusetts Institute of Technology and at Oxford in 1963–64. Dr. Searle has published numerous articles in the philosophy journals. He is currently Associate Professor of Philosophy and Special Assistant to the Chancellor at the University of California at Berkeley.

Sanford H. Kadish was born in New York City in 1921. He received his B.S.S. from the City College of New York in 1942 and his LL.B. from Columbia University in 1948. He practiced law in New York City from 1948 until 1951, when he became Professor of Law at the University of Utah. He was visiting Fulbright Professor of Law at the University of Melbourne in 1956 and visiting Professor of Law at Harvard University in 1960–61. From 1961 to 1964 he was Professor of Law at the University of Michigan. He is currently Professor of Law at the University of California at Berkeley. Mr. Kadish has published many articles and essays concerning constitutional and criminal law, and is co-author of *The Criminal Law and Its Processes*. During the fall of 1964 he was a faculty representative on the Committee on Campus Political Activity at Berkeley, and he is presently a member of the Executive Committee and the Council of the American Association of University Professors, and is Chairman of A.A.U.P. Committee A (on Academic Freedom and Tenure).

Mortimer R. Kadish was born in New York in 1917. He received a B.S.S. from the City College of New York in 1938, spent five years in the army, and attended Columbia University, where he received a Ph.D. in 1950. In 1949 he joined the faculty at Western Reserve University, where he became Chairman of the Department of Philosophy in 1957. He has taught at the University of Michigan, was recipient in 1951 of a Rockefeller Foundation Fellowship, and was a Guggenheim Fellow in 1955. In addition to articles and reviews in various journals, including *The Journal of Philosophy*, *The Philosophical Review*, and *Ethics*, Dr. Kadish has published a novel and several short stories, and has been a visiting artist at Yaddo in Saratoga Springs. From 1964 to 1966 he served as director of the WRU-Case Program of Philosophical Studies. He is currently co-director of the program, and is completing a work in aesthetics, *The Cutting Edge*.

DATE DUE

	261-2500		Printed in USA